Crystallization-Study
of the
Building of God

Volume Two

Witness Lee

The Holy Word for Morning Revival

Living Stream Ministry
Anaheim, CA • www.lsm.org

First Edition, January 2006.

ISBN 0-7363-3037-2

Published by

Living Stream Ministry

2431 W. La Palma Ave., Anaheim, CA 92801 U.S.A.

P. O. Box 2121, Anaheim, CA 92814 U.S.A.

Printed in the United States of America

06 07 08 09 10 11 12 / 10 9 8 7 6 5 4 3 2 1

Contents

Preface

1. This book is intended as an aid to believers in developing a daily time of morning revival with the Lord in His word. At the same time, it provides a partial review of the Winter Training held December 26-31, 2005, in Anaheim, California, on the crystallization-study of the building of God. Through intimate contact with the Lord in His word, the believers can be constituted with life and truth and thereby equipped to prophesy in the meetings of the church unto the building up of the Body of Christ.

2. The entire content of this book is taken from the *Crystallization-study Outlines: The Building of God,* the text and footnotes of the Recovery Version of the Bible, selections from the writings of Witness Lee and Watchman Nee, and *Hymns,* all of which are published by Living Stream Ministry.

3. The book is divided into weeks. One training message is covered per week. Each week presents first the message outline, followed by six daily portions, a hymn, and then some space for writing. The training outline has been divided into days, corresponding to the six daily portions. Each daily portion covers certain points and begins with a section entitled "Morning Nourishment." This section contains selected verses and a short reading that can provide rich spiritual nourishment through intimate fellowship with the Lord. The "Morning Nourishment" is followed by a section entitled "Today's Reading," a longer portion of ministry related to the day's main points. Each day's portion concludes with a short list of references for further reading and some space for the saints to make notes concerning their spiritual inspiration, enlightenment, and enjoyment to serve as a reminder of what they have received of the Lord that day.

4. The space provided at the end of each week is for composing a short prophecy. This prophecy can be composed by considering all of our daily notes, the "harvest" of our inspirations during the week, and preparing a main

point with some sub-points to be spoken in the church meetings for the organic building up of the Body of Christ.

5. Following the last week in this volume, we have provided a reading schedule for the New Testament Recovery Version with footnotes. This schedule is arranged so that one can read through the complete New Testament Recovery Version with footnotes in two years.

6. As a practical aid to the saints' feeding on the Word throughout the day, we have provided verse cards at the end of the volume, which correspond to each day's Scripture reading. These may be cut out and carried along as a source of spiritual enlightenment and nourishment in the saints' daily lives.

7. The *Crystallization-study Outlines* were compiled by Living Stream Ministry from the writings of Witness Lee and Watchman Nee. The outlines, footnotes, and references in the Recovery Version of the Bible are by Witness Lee. All of the other references cited in this publication are from the published ministry of Witness Lee and Watchman Nee.

Winter Training
(December 26-31, 2005)

CRYSTALLIZATION-STUDY
OF
THE BUILDING OF GOD

Banners:

The building of God is the processed Triune God
wrought into us so that
under His continual dispensing we become
His enlargement, expansion, and
corporate expression.

The three tabernacles—
the type of the tabernacle,
the reality of the tabernacle, and
the consummation of the tabernacle—
reveal the goal of God's economy
to have a corporate people
to be His dwelling place for His expression and
representation in eternity.

The intrinsic element of the work
of the divine building is to minister the building
and builded God into others
for the building up of the Body of Christ.

The desire of God's heart
is the building of God into man and
the building of man into God
for the building of a great corporate God-man,
the New Jerusalem.

The Foundation and Ground
of the Divine Building

Scripture Reading: Matt. 16:16-18; 1 Cor. 3:10-11; Rev. 1:11

Day 1
&
Day 2

I. **The foundation of the church—the divine building—is the redeeming and saving Christ, revealed and ministered through the apostles and prophets (1 Cor. 3:10-11; Eph. 2:20):**

A. As the Christ and the Son of the living God, the Lord Jesus is the unique foundation laid by God for the building of the church; no one can lay another foundation (Matt. 16:16-18; 1 Cor. 3:10-11):

1. Christ is the all-inclusive One, and nothing and no one can compare with Him (Col. 1:15-19; 2:9, 16-17; 3:4, 10-11).

2. Only Christ is qualified to be the foundation of the divine building according to God's eternal economy (1 Cor. 1:24, 30; 2:2; 3:10-11).

Day 3

B. The church is built upon the foundation of the apostles and prophets with their revelation received of Christ as the rock and with their teaching (Eph. 2:20; Matt. 16:18; Acts 2:42):

1. Because the mystery of Christ was revealed to the apostles and prophets, the revelation they received is considered the foundation on which the church is built (Eph. 3:4-5; 2:20).

2. In eternity there will be the unique New Jerusalem, built upon the foundation of many ministries laid one on top of the other, leading to the unique testimony in the unique expression (Rev. 21:14, 18-20).

3. In building the church, God works according to a prescribed and revealed plan (Matt. 16:18; Eph. 2:20; cf. Exo. 25:8-9):

a. The most important thing in our spiritual

work is a knowledge of the pattern
shown in the mountain (Heb. 8:5).

b. The pattern shown in the mountain is
God's plan; if we do not understand God's
plan, it will be impossible for us to do
God's work (Eph. 3:4).

Day 4   II. **The word *ground* that we use in reference to
the church does not carry the denotation of
a foundation; rather, it bears the denotation
of a site, like the site on which the foundation of a building is laid:**

A. According to the divine revelation in the New
Testament, the church ground is constituted of
three crucial elements:

1. The first element of the constitution of the
church ground is the unique oneness of
the universal Body of Christ (4:4):

a. This oneness is called "the oneness of the
Spirit" (v. 3).

b. This oneness is the oneness that the Lord
prayed for in John 17—a oneness in the
mingling of the processed Triune God with
all the believers in Christ (vv. 6, 11, 14-24).

c. This oneness was imparted into the
spirit of all the believers in Christ, in
their regeneration by the Spirit of life
with Christ as the divine life.

2. The second element of the constitution of
the church ground is the unique ground
of the locality in which a local church is
established and exists (Acts 14:23; Titus
1:5; Rev. 1:11).

3. The third element of the constitution of the
church ground is the reality of the Spirit
of oneness, expressing the unique oneness of the universal Body of Christ on the
unique ground of locality as a local church
(1 John 5:6; John 16:13):

a. By the Spirit of reality, who is the living

reality of the Divine Trinity, the oneness of the Body of Christ becomes real and living.

b. Through this Spirit the ground of the church is applied in life and not in legality.

c. By this Spirit the genuine ground of the church is linked with the Triune God (Eph. 4:3-6).

Day 5   B. Regarding the ground of the church, Deuteronomy 12 corresponds in at least four ways to the revelation in the New Testament:

1. In Deuteronomy 12 and in the New Testament, we see that the people of God should always be one:

   a. In His wisdom God did not allow His people to have their own choice or preference but required them to come to the unique worship center.

   b. Regardless of their number, God's children, the believers in Christ, must be one and have the same center for the worship of God.

2. Both in Deuteronomy 12 and in the New Testament, God's way to keep the oneness of His people is to have a place with His name, the unique name (Deut. 12:5, 11, 21):

   a. To be gathered into different names is to be divided, because these names are the base of divisions.

   b. Not designating ourselves by any title or name, we should be gathered together into the name of the Lord Jesus (Matt. 18:20).

3. Both Deuteronomy 12 and the New Testament reveal that the place chosen by God for our worship of Him is the place of His habitation (Deut. 12:5):

   a. The fulfillment of the type in Deuteronomy 12 is not a matter of a geographic place—it is a matter of our spirit (Eph. 2:22; John 4:21-24).

b. In gathering together for the worship of God by enjoying Christ, we must gather into the name of Christ, and we must be in the spirit; otherwise, we will lose the proper ground of the church.

Day 6
4. In Deuteronomy 12 and in the New Testament, we have the altar, the cross (Matt. 10:38):

a. At the entrance of the church is the cross, and everyone who would come into the church must experience the cross and be crucified (Gal. 6:14).

b. To experience the cross is to be set aside, to be annulled, to be reduced to nothing (1 Cor. 1:18, 23; 2:2).

5. Jeroboam's apostasy broke God's ordination of having one unique worship center in the Holy Land for keeping the oneness of the children of Israel; this apostasy can be considered a type of the apostasy in today's Christendom (1 Kings 12:25-33).

Morning Nourishment

Matt. **And Simon Peter answered and said, You are the**
16:16 **Christ, the Son of the living God.**
  18 **And I...say to you that you are Peter, and upon this**
     rock I will build My church...
1 Cor. **For another foundation no one is able to lay besides**
3:11 **that which is laid, which is Jesus Christ.**
  1:2 **To the church of God which is in Corinth, to those**
     who have been sanctified in Christ Jesus...

For the church life, there are two main and basic aspects. We must be thoroughly clear about these, for without them we have no reality of the church life. The first is that Christ Himself is the life, the content, and everything in the church. It is absolutely not a matter of forms, doctrines, or certain kinds of expressions. Those who are really in the church life are those who are experiencing Christ as their very life day by day. Christ is everything to them; therefore, Christ is their life and content whenever they come together. The practice of the church life is a life of Christ and a life with Christ as everything. The second main aspect of the church life is that of the standing or the ground of the church. (*The Ground of the Church*, p. 1)

Today's Reading

The ground of the church is not the foundation of the church. The foundation of the church is Christ...(1 Cor. 3:11). The ground is completely different from the foundation. The foundation is a basic and integral part of the construction of a building, whereas the ground is not. The ground is a piece of land, called the site, upon which the foundation is laid....We must not mistake the ground for the foundation or the foundation for the ground. They are two vital yet distinct entities for the construction of a building. Although the foundation may be deeply embedded in the ground, it is still distinct and separate from it. The ground is the standing on which the foundation is laid.

When Paul went to Corinth and brought people to the Lord, he established the church in Corinth. Upon what ground? Upon the ground of Corinth. He set up a local church in Corinth with Christ as its foundation upon the unique ground of locality. When Apollos went to Corinth, he did not set up another church. He built up the saints upon the same unique foundation and upon the same unique ground, the ground of Corinth. Paul planted them on that ground, and Apollos watered them on that ground. First Corinthians 1:2 says, "The church [singular] of God which is in Corinth." Paul, Apollos, and Peter brought their varied ministries to Corinth, but they all built *one* church with *one* foundation upon the *one* ground of unity. So eventually only one church existed in Corinth with one kind of saints, one foundation which is Christ, and one ground which was the common standing in the entire locality. One church, one foundation, one ground—it is so clear.

The problem today is not with the foundation but with the ground. This is why we say that if we would have the church life, we must consider the ground as the second essential point we must take into account. Without Christ as our life and content and without the ground of unity with the saints in the locality in which we live as our definite standing, we cannot practice the church life.

The Scriptures clearly show us that in every locality the expression of the Body of Christ, that is, the local church, should be just one. There is no place in the Scriptures where there was more than one local church in any given city. If you are living in Los Angeles, you must be built up together with other believers in Los Angeles...as the unique local church there, which should be called the church in [Los Angeles]. The one that was built up in Jerusalem was called the church in Jerusalem (Acts 8:1), and the one in Antioch was called the church in Antioch (Acts 13:1). In the same principle, the one in Los Angeles should be called the church in Los Angeles....Wherever we live, we are the church in that place and we build the church in that place. If all God's people could see this principle and abide by it, there would be no divisions. (*The Ground of the Church,* pp. 2, 5-6, 8-9)

Further Reading: The Ground of the Church; The Practical Expression of the Church, ch. 6

Enlightenment and inspiration: _____

_____

_____

_____

Morning Nourishment

1 Cor. **According to the grace of God given to me, as a**
3:10 **wise master builder I have laid a foundation, and**
another builds upon *it.* **But let each man take heed**
how he builds upon *it.*
12 **But if anyone builds upon the foundation gold,**
silver, precious stones, wood, grass, stubble.

In God's building Christ is the unique foundation...(1 Cor.
3:11). As the Christ and the Son of the living God, the Lord Jesus
Christ is the unique foundation laid by God for His building. No
one can lay any other foundation. Christ is the all-inclusive One.
Nothing and no one can compare with Him. Nothing and no one,
other than He, is qualified to be the foundation of the divine building in the universe according to God's eternal economy. He is the
unique One to be the unique foundation of this divine building.
(*The Conclusion of the New Testament,* p. 639)

Today's Reading

Doctrinally speaking, many Christians understand what it
means not to lay any foundation other than Jesus Christ. However, when writing [1 Corinthians 3:10-11], Paul was not speaking in a doctrinal way. He realized that by saying that they were of
Paul, Apollos, or Cephas, the Corinthians were actually laying
another foundation. Here Paul seems to be saying, "Believers at
Corinth, you should not say that you are of anyone or of anything.
Christ, the unique foundation, has already been laid....This
Christ is the unique foundation."

It is common for Christians to lay foundations other than
Christ as the unique foundation. For example, when someone
declares that he is for immersion, he is laying immersion as a
foundation. The same is true of someone who is for tongues-
speaking. Whenever you claim to be for a particular person, doctrine, or practice, you are laying another foundation. This is the
right meaning of Paul's word in verses 10 and 11.

Christians have been divided by the many different foundations. Thousands of foundations have been laid, and more are

being laid. Thus, we should be careful not to say that we are of a certain thing or of a certain person. To speak in this way is to lay another foundation; it is also to cause division....We are only of Christ and for Christ....Regarding this matter, my eyes are very watchful, not over Christianity, but over the Lord's recovery. Even the saints who love the Lord and His recovery may still say that they are for certain things. This is to lay another foundation.

Instead of laying another foundation, we must build upon the foundation already laid. This means that we must build upon the unique Christ. We should understand this not only doctrinally, but also practically and experientially. For example, suppose a brother tells you that, according to his feeling, the church in your locality is not positive. How would you respond to this? The answer you give will reveal whether or not you are building upon Christ as the unique foundation. The best way to respond is not to correct the brother or argue with him, but to pray-read a few verses with him....If you pray-read together instead of discussing the situation, that one will be watered and nourished. Nothing waters others and nourishes others more than your living spirit.

To fellowship with others with a living spirit full of the riches of Christ is to build upon Christ as the unique foundation. It is also to build with Christ. When you contact others in this way, you build upon Christ and with Christ. As a result, others will be solidly built up into the church as part of the Body. This is to build upon the foundation already laid.

We must take heed not to build with anything other than Christ. This means that whenever we give a message or a testimony, or whenever we have fellowship with others, we must be careful not to give others anything except Christ. Furthermore, the Christ we share should not be a doctrinal Christ, but a Christ whom we have experienced. (*Life-study of 1 Corinthians,* pp. 229-232)

Further Reading: Life-study of 1 Corinthians, msg. 26; *The Conclusion of the New Testament,* msg. 59

Enlightenment and inspiration: _____

_____

_____

_____

Morning Nourishment

Eph. Being built upon the foundation of the apostles and
2:20 prophets, Christ Jesus Himself being the cornerstone.
3:4-5 ...You can perceive my understanding in the mystery
of Christ, which in other generations was not made
known to the sons of men, as it has now been revealed
to His holy apostles and prophets in spirit.

Ephesians 2:20 speaks of the foundation of the apostles and prophets. This foundation is the very Christ whom they ministered to others. Paul said that Christ was the unique foundation which he had laid. No one can lay another foundation (1 Cor. 3:10-11). The Christ who is the foundation of the church is the unique Christ revealed and ministered by the early apostles, as recorded in the New Testament. (*The Basic Revelation in the Holy Scriptures*, p. 69)

Today's Reading

As the Body of Christ, the church has been regenerated, and as the house of God, the church is being built....The building of the house is the growth of the Body. If the Body does not grow, the house cannot be built.

In considering the church as God's building, we need to pay special attention to the foundation....Many Christians have difficulty understanding what the foundation is in Ephesians 2:20. First Corinthians 3:11 says, "For another foundation no one is able to lay besides that which is laid, which is Jesus Christ.." Christ is the only foundation. Nevertheless, Ephesians 2:20 speaks of the foundation of the apostles and prophets. This does not mean, however, that the apostles and prophets themselves are the foundation. In contrast to Revelation 21 where the foundations are the very persons of the apostles, the foundation here is not the apostles and prophets themselves. Since the mystery of Christ has been revealed to the apostles (Eph. 3:4-5), the revelation they received is considered the foundation upon which the church is built. This corresponds to the rock in Matthew 16:18, which is not only Christ Himself but also the revelation concerning Christ, upon which Christ will build His church. Therefore, the foundation of the apostles and prophets is the revelation they received regarding Christ and the church for the building of the church. The church is built upon this revelation. This is the meaning of the foundation in Ephesians 2:20.

Upon what are we in the Lord's recovery building the church? To say that we are building upon Christ is too vague and indefinite. We need to build the church upon the revelation received by the apostles and prophets. The so-called churches established according to nationalities are not built upon the foundation of the apostles and prophets. Some so-called churches even exclude members of particular racial or ethnic groups. Surely those congregations are not built upon the foundation spoken of in 2:20. The Roman Catholic Church and all the denominations claim that their foundation is Christ. However, none of these groups declares that their foundation is the foundation of the apostles and prophets. For example, the Presbyterian denomination is built upon the concept of presbytery. The apostles and prophets, however, never received a revelation that the presbytery should be the foundation of the church. The Methodist Church is built upon the principles of John Wesley, and the Catholic Church is built upon the concept of hierarchy. If the revelation given to the apostles and prophets were applied to the Catholic Church, the Catholic Church would collapse. The charismatic churches are built upon the foundation of certain charismatic gifts and experiences. In contrast to all these so-called churches, we in the Lord's recovery must be able to strongly affirm that the churches in the recovery are built upon the foundation of the apostles and prophets. This means that the churches in the Lord's recovery are built according to the revelation received by the apostles and prophets. This revelation embraces believers of all races and nationalities; it includes those who speak in tongues and those who do not. If you have the vision of the proper foundation of the church, you will realize that only the churches in the Lord's recovery...are built upon the proper foundation. (*Life-study of Ephesians*, pp. 233-235)

Further Reading: The Basic Revelation in the Holy Scriptures, ch. 5; *Life-study of Ephesians*, msg. 27

Enlightenment and inspiration: _____

_____

_____

_____

Morning Nourishment

Eph. Being diligent to keep the oneness of the Spirit in the
4:3-4 uniting bond of peace: one Body and one Spirit, even
as also you were called in one hope of your calling.
John That they all may be one; even as You, Father, are in
17:21-23 Me and I in You, that they also may be in Us; that the
world may believe that You have sent Me. And the
glory which You have given Me I have given to them,
that they may be one, even as We are one; I in them,
and You in Me, that they may be perfected into one...

The word *ground* that we use in reference to the church
ground...bears the denotation of a site, like the site on which the
foundation of a building is laid....According to the divine revelation of the New Testament, the church ground is constituted of
three crucial elements, as follows:

The first element of the constitution of the church ground is
the unique oneness of the universal Body of Christ, which is
called "the oneness of the Spirit" (Eph. 4:3). This is the oneness
that the Lord prayed for in John 17. It is a oneness of the mingling
of the processed Triune God with all the believers in Christ. This
oneness is in the name of the Father (John 17:6, 11), denoting the
Father's person, in which is the Father's life. This oneness is even
in the Triune God through sanctification by His holy word as the
truth (John 17:14-21). This oneness is ultimately in the divine
glory for the expression of the Triune God (John 17:22-24). Such a
oneness was imparted into the spirit of all the believers in Christ,
in their regeneration by the Spirit of life with Christ as the divine
life; this oneness has become the basic element of the church
ground. (*A Brief Presentation of the Lord's Recovery,* p. 28)

Today's Reading

The second element of the church ground is the unique ground
of the locality in which a local church is established and exists.
The New Testament presents us a clear picture that all the local
churches, as the expression of the universal church—the universal Body of Christ—are located in their respective cities. Hence,

we see the church in Jerusalem (Acts 8:1), the church in Antioch (Acts 13:1), the church in Cenchrea (Rom. 16:1), the church in Corinth (1 Cor. 1:2), and the seven churches in Asia in seven respective cities (Rev. 1:4, 11). Every city as the boundary in which a church exists is the local ground of that church. Such a unique ground of locality preserves the church from being divided by many different matters as different grounds.

The third element of the church ground is the reality of the Spirit of oneness, expressing the unique oneness of the universal Body of Christ on the unique ground of locality of a local church.... The reality of the Spirit...is the living reality of the Divine Trinity (1 John 5:6; John 16:13). It is by this Spirit that the oneness of the Body of Christ becomes real and living. It is also through this Spirit that the ground of locality is applied in life and not in legality. And it is by this Spirit that the genuine ground of the church is linked with the Triune God (Eph. 4:3-6).

The above-defined ground of the church keeps, in practicality, the genuine oneness of the church both locally and universally (Eph. 4:3), without any division. This is the only way to avoid today's situation of division and confusion among the members of Christ.

The above-defined ground of the church is also the base of the genuine and proper fellowship of all the believers, which is called "the fellowship of the apostles" in the divine revelation (Acts 2:42), a fellowship that is with the Triune God and with all the members of Christ (1 John 1:1-3). This is the unique fellowship of the Body of Christ locally and universally. Because of the many divisive grounds of today's Christianity, the fellowship among the members of Christ also is divided into many divisive fellowships. The way to be saved out of all these divisive fellowships is to take and keep the unique, genuine, and proper ground of the church. This is not a matter of doctrine and regulation; it is a spiritual fact and a practical necessity. (*A Brief Presentation of the Lord's Recovery,* pp. 28-30)

Further Reading: A Brief Presentation of the Lord's Recovery, pp. 25-56; *The Ground of the Church and the Meetings of the Church,* ch. 1

Enlightenment and inspiration: _____

_____

_____

_____

Morning Nourishment

Deut. But to the place which Jehovah your God will
12:5 choose out of all your tribes to put His name, to His
habitation, shall you seek, and there shall you go.

11 Then to the place where Jehovah your God will
choose to cause His name to dwell, there you shall
bring all that I am commanding you, your burnt
offerings and your sacrifices, your tithes and the
heave offering of your hand and all your choice
vows which you vow to Jehovah.

Eph. In whom you also are being built together into a
2:22 dwelling place of God in spirit.

Chapter twelve of Deuteronomy corresponds in at least four
ways to the revelation in the New Testament. First, both in this
chapter and in the New Testament we see that the people of God
should always be one. In order to preserve the oneness of the children of Israel, God did not allow each of the twelve tribes to have its
own worship center. If each tribe had had its own center for the worship of God, there would have been twelve divisions among God's
people, for each center would have been the ground and the base of a
division. In His wisdom, God did not allow His people to have their
own choice or preference but required them to take His choice and
to come three times a year to the unique worship center, even
though travel to that place was inconvenient for many of them.

The principle is the same in the New Testament. Regardless of
their number, God's children, the believers in Christ, must be one
and have the same center for the worship of God. However, the
actual situation among Christians today is division. There are
many worship centers, and this has led to divisions. (*Life-study of
Deuteronomy*, pp. 73-74)

Today's Reading

Whenever the believers have their own way and their own
preference, there will be division. All denominations are according to man's preferences. The situation in the Lord's recovery is
altogether different. The Lord's recovery is a matter of coming

back to God's way according to God's preference.

Second, both in Deuteronomy 12 and in the New Testament, God's way to keep the oneness of His people is to have a place with His name, the unique name. The name in which we gather for the worship of God is a matter of great importance. We should never think that it is insignificant. Today Christians should be gathered together into only one name, the name of the Lord Jesus (Matt. 18:20). However, Christians are accustomed to being gathered into other names, such as Baptist, Presbyterian, Episcopalian, Lutheran, and Methodist. To be gathered into these different names is to be divided, because these names are the base of divisions.

To have other names for our worship is an abomination; it is spiritual fornication. We are Christ's counterpart, His wife....We should not have a name other than His name. To take another name is to take another person. Just as a wife should bear the name of her husband, not the name of any other man, so we, the believers in Christ, should bear only His name and not any other name....Like the church in Philadelphia, we should not deny the Lord's name (Rev. 3:8); that is, we should abandon all names other than that of the Lord Jesus Christ,...[and] simply be gathered together into the name of the Lord.

Third,...the place chosen by God for our worship of Him is the place of His habitation....According to Ephesians 2:22, God's habitation, His dwelling place, is in our spirit. Yes, as a church we should be gathered into the name of Christ, but we also need to be exercised in our spirit. If we come together under the name of Christ but, instead of exercising our spirit, we remain in the natural mind or, even worse, in the flesh, we will not be in the habitation of God. In gathering together for the worship of God by enjoying Christ, we must gather into the name of Christ and we must be in the spirit. Otherwise, we will lose the proper ground of the church. (*Life-study of Deuteronomy,* pp. 74-75)

Further Reading: Life-study of Deuteronomy, msg. 10; *Young People's Training,* ch. 13

Enlightenment and inspiration: _____

_____
_____
_____

Morning Nourishment

Matt.   And he who does not take his cross and follow after
10:38 Me is not worthy of Me.
1 Cor. For I did not determine to know anything among
2:2   you except Jesus Christ, and this One crucified.
Gal.   But far be it from me to boast except in the cross of
6:14   our Lord Jesus Christ, through whom the world
      has been crucified to me and I to the world.

Concerning our meeting for the worship of God, we all must learn two crucial things. First, we must learn to reject every name other than the name of the Lord Jesus and to be gathered into His name. Second, we must learn to reject the flesh, the self, and the natural life and to exercise our spirit. In everything related to the worship of God, we need to exercise our spirit. Whenever we sing, we should sing with our spirit. Whenever we praise, we should praise with our spirit. Whenever we speak, we should speak with our spirit. If we do this, the meeting will be in God's habitation. (*Life-study of Deuteronomy*, p. 75)

Today's Reading

[As in Deuteronomy 12, today] we have the altar, the cross. Along with the name and the habitation, we must have the altar, which signifies the cross. Paul's word in 1 Corinthians 2:2 indicates the importance of this....The crucified Christ was the unique subject, the center, the content, and the substance of Paul's ministry.

At the entrance of the church is the cross, and everyone who would come into the church must experience the cross and be crucified. To experience the cross is to be set aside, to be annulled, to be reduced to nothing. In the church there should be only Christ, not us....We should be on the cross....We should not bring anything of the old man, anything of the flesh, the self, or the natural life, into the church. When we are on the cross, we are truly in the spirit.

As we are preparing to come to the meeting, we may pray, "Lord, if I still have something related to the flesh, the self, and the natural life, I ask You to forgive me and to cross out these things. Lord, I need to be crossed out and then anointed with Yourself." If we all come to the meeting in this way, we will meet in the name of Christ, we will meet in God's habitation, and we will meet under the application of the cross.

If we have the name, the habitation, and the cross, there will be no divisions among us....We all will be one—one in the same name, one in the same habitation, and one under the same cross. (*Life-study of Deuteronomy,* pp. 75-76)

After the death of Solomon, the kingdom of David was divided ...(1 Kings 11:29-37). From that time onward, the children of Israel were two separate kingdoms—the kingdom of Judah to the south and the kingdom of Israel to the north. The worship center chosen by God, however, was not divided; it was still one....Jeroboam was very concerned about this matter. Probably deep in his heart, he said, "If these ten tribes continue going to Jerusalem to worship the Lord, they may be influenced to kill me and to return to the house of David." Therefore, Jeroboam set up two other worship centers, one in Bethel and one in Dan, for the convenience of his people (1 Kings 12:26-33). Jeroboam seemed to be saying to the people in a subtle way: "It is too far for you to travel to Jerusalem. It is not at all convenient. I have set up two other worship centers for you. Now you don't need to go to Jerusalem. You may go either to Dan or to Bethel to worship your God."

The significance of Jeroboam's sin can be seen in practice in today's Christianity. Certain pastors and so-called Christian workers desire to have an empire under their control. In order to have their own kingdom, they, like Jeroboam, establish their own worship centers. Jeroboam did not have the real God. [He] made two calves of gold....Just as Jeroboam had God only in name, some of the things that are called "God" in the worship centers today are simply God in name. Actually, it is not God—it is a calf. (*Young People's Training,* pp. 160-161)

Further Reading: Young People's Training, ch. 12; Life-study of 1 & 2 Kings, msg. 8

Enlightenment and inspiration: _____

_____

_____

_____

Hymns, #1251

1 To Jerusalem we've come,
    We are through with Babylon,
    We have gathered to be one,
      O glory be to God!
    Of the teachings we're bereft,
    All opinions we have left,
    Spirit from the soul is cleft,
    In the local churches now.

      Hallelujah! Hallelujah!
      We are all in one accord
      For the building of the Lord.
      Hallelujah! Hallelujah!
      We are living in the local
        churches now!

2 That recovery may proceed
    Real priests are what we need—
    Those who live in Christ indeed,
      O glory be to God!
    Saturated with the Lord,
    They have Christ as their reward.
    These the building work afford
    In the local churches now.

3 And the kingship we must see
    With divine authority—
    To this rule we'll all agree,
      O glory be to God!
    To the Spirit we'll submit
    For the church's benefit—
    This is His prerequisite
    In the local churches now.

4 We the altar must obtain,
    Have our all upon it lain.
    The burnt-offering must be slain,
      O glory be to God!
    This we never should dispute,
    For the church be absolute,
    All that's otherwise uproot
    In the local churches now.

5   The foundation now is laid—
    O what glory doth pervade!
    We are all with joy arrayed,
        O glory be to God!
    Let us raise a mighty shout—
    They will hear us far without,
    And the enemy we'll rout
        In the local churches now.

Composition for prophecy with main point and sub-points: _____

_____

_____

_____

_____

_____

_____

_____

_____

_____

_____

_____

_____

_____

_____

_____

_____

_____

_____

_____

_____

_____

_____

_____

_____

_____

_____

_____

_____

_____

_____

_____

The Materials of the Divine Building

Scripture Reading: Gen. 2:10-12; Exo. 28:29; S. S. 1:10-11; 3:9-10; 1 Cor. 3:12; Rev. 21:18-21

Day 1
&
Day 2

I. **The materials of the divine building are the processed and consummated Triune God and His transformed believers, who have been united, mingled, and incorporated with Him to be a miraculous structure of treasure for the universal display of the surpassing riches of His grace with His infinite wisdom and divine design (Matt. 16:18; Eph. 2:7; 3:8-11).**

II. **Genesis 2 reveals God's architectural plan to build Himself into us as precious materials for the building of the New Jerusalem (Heb. 11:10):**

A. God created man as a vessel with a human spirit to contain Him as life (Gen. 2:7; Rom. 9:21, 23; 2 Cor. 4:7; 2 Tim. 2:21).

B. God placed man in front of the tree of life, which signifies the Triune God embodied in Christ as life to man in the form of food (Gen. 2:9).

C. The river going forth from Eden signifies the river of water of life flowing forth from God as the source of the living water for man to drink (v. 10; Rev. 22:1).

D. The flow of the river issues in three precious materials, which typify the Triune God as the basic elements of the structure of God's eternal building (Gen. 2:12; Rev. 21:11, 18-21):

1. Gold typifies God the Father with His divine nature as the base of God's eternal building (2 Pet. 1:4).

2. Bdellium, a pearl-like material produced from the resin of a tree, typifies the produce of God the Son in His redeeming and life-releasing death and His life-dispensing

resurrection as the entry into God's eternal building (John 19:34; 12:24; cf. Rev. 21:21).

　　3. Onyx, a precious stone, typifies the produce of God the Spirit with His transforming work for the building up of God's eternal building (2 Cor. 3:18; Rom. 12:2).

Day 3　　E. The flowing of the divine life in man brings the divine nature into man, regenerates man, and transforms man into precious materials for God's building, which will consummate in the New Jerusalem as the ultimate and eternal Eve, the corporate bride, the wife of the Lamb (Gen. 2:22; 2 Pet. 1:4; 1 Pet. 1:3; 2 Cor. 3:18; Rev. 21:9; 22:17).

Day 4　III. **The twelve precious stones on the breast-plate of the high priest signify all the redeemed and transformed people of God built together to become one entity (Exo. 28:15-30):**

　　A. The twelve precious stones set in gold symbolize the saints as transformed precious stones built together in the divine nature of Christ to become one entity, the church as Christ's Body (vv. 17-20).

　　B. As components of the church, we must be transformed in our human nature to become precious stones for God's eternal building through the burning and pressure in our environment and the flowing of the divine life in our being.

　　C. The breastplate being borne upon Aaron's heart for a memorial before Jehovah signifies the entire church as one built-up entity being borne upon Christ's loving heart for a memorial, a pleasing remembrance, before God (v. 29).

　IV. **Song of Songs 1:10-11 reveals that Christ's lover is transformed with the Triune God's attributes by the remaking Spirit in coordination with the lover's companions, the gifted members in the Body of Christ:**

A. The seeker's hair being bound into plaits of gold indicates her submission to God through the transformation of the Spirit with God the Father in His divine nature.

B. The plaits of gold are fastened with studs of silver, signifying Christ the Son in His all-inclusive judicial redemption.

C. The strings of jewels on the seeker's neck signify God the Spirit in His transforming work to become her obedience to God's will.

V. **Song of Songs 3:9-10 reveals that we are rebuilt with the Triune God by the Spirit's transforming work in us to become a palanquin of Christ for the move of Christ in and for the Body of Christ:**

A. We are rebuilt with the Triune God so that our external structure is the resurrected and ascended humanity of Jesus (wood of Lebanon), and our interior decoration is our love for the Lord (inlaid with love) (2 Cor. 5:14).

B. Through our loving the Lord in a personal, affectionate, private, and spiritual way, our natural being is torn down, and we are remodeled with Christ in His redeeming death (its posts, made of silver), with God in His divine nature (its base, of gold), and with Christ as the life-giving Spirit ruling within us in His kingship (its seat, of purple) (Rom. 8:28-29; 2 Cor. 4:16-18).

Day 5
&
Day 6

VI. **The church in the New Testament is "God's cultivated land, God's building" (1 Cor. 3:9) and is built with gold, silver, and precious stones (v. 12a):**

A. The believers, who have been regenerated in Christ with God's life, are God's cultivated land, a farm in God's new creation to grow Christ so that precious materials may be produced for God's building.

B. Gold, silver, and precious stones signify the various experiences of Christ in the virtues and attributes of the Triune God; silver, signifying Christ's redemption, is listed instead of bdellium or pearl because of man's need of redemption after the fall.

C. Wood, in contrast to gold, signifies the nature of the natural man; grass, in contrast to silver, signifies the fallen man, the man of the flesh (1 Pet. 1:24); and stubble, in contrast to precious stones, signifies the work and living that issue from an earthen source; all these are not worthy to be used as materials for the divine building (1 Cor. 3:12b).

VII. **The New Jerusalem as the greatest and ultimate sign in the Scriptures is an organic constitution of the processed Triune God mingled with His regenerated, transformed, and glorified tripartite elect (Rev. 21:2, 9-10):**

A. Its base is pure gold, signifying the divine nature of God; it is the solid foundation of its throne for the divine administration, which is the glorious center from which proceeds the divine and human communication, signified by its street, to reach all its twelve gates (vv. 18b, 21b; 22:1-2).

B. Its gates are pearls, signifying the issue of the secretion of Christ's redeeming and life-releasing death and His life-dispensing resurrection (21:12b-13, 21a).

C. Its wall and its foundations are precious stones, consummated by the Spirit through His transforming and building work (vv. 18a, 19-20).

S. S.

1:10 Your cheeks are lovely w/ plaits of ornaments, your neck w/ strings of jewels.

11 We will make you plaits of gold w/ studs of silver.

Morning Nourishment

Gen. And a river went forth from Eden to water the gar-
2:10-12 den, and from there it divided and became four
branches. The name of the first is Pishon; it is the
one that goes around the whole land of Havilah,
where there is gold. And the gold of that land is
good; bdellium and onyx stone are there.

Rev. And the building work of its wall was jasper; and
21:18-19 the city was pure gold, like clear glass. The foundations of the wall of the city were adorned with every
precious stone: the first foundation was jasper...
21 And the twelve gates were twelve pearls...

The flow of the river issued in three precious materials: gold,
bdellium, and onyx. These materials typify the Triune God as the
basic elements of the structure of God's eternal building. Gold typifies God the Father with His divine nature, which man may partake of through God's calling (2 Pet. 1:3-4), as the base of God's
eternal building; bdellium, a pearl-like material produced from the
resin of a tree, typifies the produce of God the Son in His redeeming
and life-releasing death (John 19:34) and His life-dispensing resurrection (John 12:24; 1 Pet. 1:3), as the entry into God's eternal
building (cf. Rev. 21:21 and note 1, par. 1); and onyx, a precious
stone, typifies the produce of God the Spirit with His transforming
work (2 Cor. 3:18) for the building up of God's eternal building. The
New Jerusalem is constructed of these three categories of materials—gold, pearl, and precious stones (Rev. 21:11, 18-21).

The breastplate of the high priest, a symbol of Israel as God's
Old Testament people, was constructed of gold and precious stones
(Exo. 28:6-21), and the church in the New Testament is built with
gold, silver, and precious stones (1 Cor. 3:12...). This indicates that
the New Jerusalem includes the totality of God's chosen and redeemed people—Israel plus the church. (Gen. 2:12, note 1)

Today's Reading

We also need to pay attention to a very crucial word in the New
Testament—transformation....Transformation is not a mere

outward change; it is an organic change, a metabolic change. Transformation means to change a substance from one form and element into another form and element. Precious stones are produced by such a process of transformation.

The eternal purpose of God...is to express Himself and to exercise His dominion through man. For the fulfillment of this purpose, God created man in a specific way as a vessel to contain God Himself as life. Thus, God created man with a human spirit that he might contact God, receive God, retain God, and assimilate God into his whole being. After creating man in this way, God placed him in a garden with the tree of life as the center. Near the tree of life was a river flowing,...[which] brings forth gold, pearl [or bdellium], and onyx stone. The setting for all of this is a garden, and a garden signifies the natural things created by God. In a garden we can see the growth of created things.

When we come to Revelation 21 and 22, we do not find a garden, but a city. A city is not created; it is built. In Genesis 2 we have creation; in Revelation 21 and 22 we have the building. In the city we also have the tree of life. Thus, the Bible begins and ends with life. Moreover, in the city we find a river of living water proceeding out of the throne of God. This corresponds to the river in the garden. Furthermore, in Revelation we find the three categories of precious materials, not in a natural state, but built into a city made with gold, pearl, and precious stones. Therefore, what was sown in Genesis as a seed is reaped in Revelation as the harvest.

Between the garden and the city a long process must transpire, and a great deal of work must be accomplished. Nevertheless, the seed sown in the garden becomes the harvest in the city. This seed includes the tree of life, a river of water, and the three precious materials. At the time of harvest in Revelation, the materials are no longer in a natural state, but become a building fitly joined together. The New Jerusalem is a building of gold, pearl, and precious stones. (*Life-study of Genesis,* pp. 147-149)

Further Reading: Life-study of Genesis, msg. 12

Enlightenment and inspiration: _____

_____

_____

_____

Morning Nourishment

1 Cor. According to the grace of God given to me, as a wise
3:10-12 master builder I have laid a foundation, and another
builds upon *it*. But let each man take heed how he
builds upon *it*. For another foundation no one is able
to lay besides that which is laid, which is Jesus
Christ. But if anyone builds upon the foundation
gold, silver, precious stones, wood, grass, stubble.

Exo. And you shall enclose in [the breasplate] enclosures
28:17 of stones, four rows of stones...

21 And the stones shall be according to the names of the
sons of Israel,...*like* the engravings of a signet,...for
the twelve tribes.

In 1 Corinthians 3 Paul says that as a master builder he laid the
unique foundation, Jesus Christ, and that we all must take heed
how we build upon it. What materials are we using in building up
the church? Paul tells us to build with gold, silver, and precious
stones. (Later we will see why he substituted silver for pearl.) By this
we can see that not only the New Jerusalem is built with gold, pearl,
and precious stones, but even the church in this age must be built
with gold, silver, and precious stones, not with wood, grass, and stubble. As we shall see, gold contrasts with wood, silver opposes grass,
and precious stones are versus stubble. (*Life-study of Genesis*, p. 150)

Today's Reading

When I saw this as a young Christian, I was excited. I saw a
garden in Genesis 2 with precious materials. I saw a city in Revelation built with these same materials. Between Genesis and Revelation I saw a church built with gold, silver, and precious stones. I
saw that the church is a composition of all the redeemed people,
and that this composition is a building....We, God's redeemed people, are the materials for His spiritual building.

In Old Testament times God also had a people, the children of
Israel. The most prominent person among them was the high
priest who represented them in the presence of God. Whenever he
went into the presence of God on behalf of the people, he had to

wear two shoulder plates and a breastplate. On the shoulder plates were two large pieces of onyx stone on which were engraved the names of the twelve tribes of Israel. On the breastplate was a beautiful setting of fine, inlaid gold, and within this setting were set twelve precious stones in four rows of three stones each. The twelve stones in the breastplate correspond to the number twelve in the New Jerusalem....In Revelation 21 we find the names of these twelve tribes on the twelve gates of the city. This is very significant.

In the New Testament we have a church built with gold, silver, and precious stones. In the Old Testament we have God's people composed with gold and precious stones to become a complete entity. In the eyes of God, the breastplate of the high priest was a part of the miniature of the coming New Jerusalem. Likewise, the church built with gold, silver, and precious stones is also a part of the miniature of the New Jerusalem. In the Old Testament we have Israel with twelve tribes. In the New Testament we have the church with twelve apostles. Hence, Israel plus the church equals the New Jerusalem....This building covers the entire Bible from... a garden in Genesis to...a city in Revelation. Between the garden and the city are two peoples, Israel and the church....Eventually, all of these have been transformed into gold, silver or pearl, and precious stones. Hence, the garden, the city, and the two peoples are all related to the three categories of precious materials.

In the Bible, between the garden and the city, there are not only the two peoples...as God's dwelling place, but there are also the life and the river enjoyed by these two peoples. Psalm 36:8-9 tells us that the children of Israel enjoyed the fountain of life and the river of pleasures in God. John 6 and 7 point out that the people in the church enjoy the bread of life and the rivers of living water. Hence, in the Bible there is the continued mention not only of the precious materials but also of the life and river mentioned at the beginning and at the end. (*Life-study of Genesis,* pp. 150-151)

Further Reading: Life-study of Genesis, msg. 12; *Life and Building as Portrayed in the Song of Songs,* chs. 4-6

Enlightenment and inspiration: _____

_____

_____

_____

Morning Nourishment

1 Cor.   But if anyone builds upon the foundation gold, silver,
3:12   precious stones, wood, grass, stubble.

2 Pet.   Through which He has granted to us precious and
1:4   exceedingly great promises that through these you
       might become partakers of the divine nature...

Why is pearl [or bdellium] found in Genesis 2 and Revelation 21 and silver in 1 Corinthians 3? In 1 Corinthians 3 we have silver because in typology silver represents redemption. The meaning of redemption is to deal with sin. If there had been no sin, there would have been no need of redemption. In the garden of Genesis 2 there was no sin, and for eternity in the New Jerusalem of Revelation 21 sin will be banished. Sin came in from Genesis 3 and will be fully eliminated in Revelation 20. Thus, in neither Genesis 2 nor Revelation 21 do we find sin. Therefore, in these situations there is no need for redemption, for silver. The need there is not silver for redemption, but pearl for regeneration. Redemption is to take away sin; regeneration is to bring in the divine life. Silver stands for redemption between Genesis 2 and Revelation 21 because of the great problem of sin that necessitates redemption. In the present age we need silver. (*Life-study of Genesis*, pp. 151-152)

Today's Reading

With all of this as a background, we come to the subject of transformation. We have seen that God has a purpose, and for the fulfillment of His purpose He created man as a vessel to contain Him, making him with a human spirit…to contact and worship Him.

God is life. God Himself is the tree of life. When He came in the flesh, He revealed Himself as life and as the life supply. Christ is the bread of life (John 6:35). Whatever we take into us as food will be assimilated into our being. This is very meaningful and significant. God is life to us in the form of food. We need to receive Him by eating Him. Once God enters into us, He becomes the flow of life within us. For proper eating we need food and drink. John 6 covers the bread of life for our eating, and John 7 covers the living water for our drinking.…In Genesis 2 we have the tree of life for our food and the flowing river for our drink....When we take in the Lord as our food, we will also have Him as the water flowing within us.

The flow of living water brings forth three kinds of materials. The first of these is gold, which typifies God's divine nature.... Gold itself is not a transformed substance; it is an element. Unlike gold, pearl and precious stones are transformed materials, for they have been changed from one form into another. Gold is a created element and can never be transformed or changed....[It] is precious, expensive, and valuable. Thus, in typology God used gold to signify His divine nature. This divine nature has been brought into our being. The element of gold has been added to us (2 Pet. 1:4; 1 Cor. 3:12; Rev. 21:18, 21).

Gold is weighty. Before you prayed [for a period of time], you were light and loose. However, after praying for two hours, you have an element in you that is precious, shining, and weighty....When you pray to God the Father or call on the name of the Lord Jesus, the divine life flows within you to bring forth gold.

How much "gold" do you have within you?...If we pray and walk in the spirit, the inner gold will increase daily. The flow of the divine life will add more of the divine nature to us. Although we were made of clay, God's intention is to impart His gold into us by the flow of His life. In this way the process of transformation begins.

Transformation requires a new element to be added to the original element. Suppose I am a person with a pale complexion. If you color my face with make-up, that is outward beautification, not inward transformation. If I am to have a real change, a new element must be added to me. How can it be added? By my eating. If I eat healthy meals day after day, I will undergo an inward transformation, an inward metabolic change in life. When a metabolic change occurs, new elements are added and old elements are discharged. This is transformation. (*Life-study of Genesis*, pp. 152-154)

Further Reading: Life and Building as Portrayed in the Song of Songs, chs. 4-6; *The Application of the Interpretation of the New Jerusalem to the Seeking Believers*, ch. 1

Enlightenment and inspiration: _____

_____

_____

_____

Morning Nourishment

Matt. And finding one pearl of great value, he went and
13:46 sold all that he had and bought it.
Rev. ...The twelve gates were twelve pearls; each one of the
21:21 gates was, respectively, of one pearl. And the street of
the city was pure gold, like transparent glass.
18 And the building work of its wall was jasper...

What does the pearl signify? Although pearl is replaced with silver in 1 Corinthians because of the need for redemption, pearl was God's original concept.

Consider how a pearl is formed. An oyster living in the sea is wounded by a piece of sand. The oyster secretes life juice around the grain of sand until the sand becomes a pearl. Christ is the oyster who lived in the ocean of this world. We are the grains of sand that wound Him and, after injuring Him, stay at His wound. His life secretes His life essence, enveloping us with it layer upon layer. Eventually, after becoming fully enclosed by this life-secretion, we become a pearl (Matt. 13:46). This is the experience of regeneration. Originally, we were small pieces of sand, but we became pearls as the life juice of Christ enveloped our being. Every gate of the New Jerusalem is a pearl, signifying the entrance into the kingdom of God (Rev. 21:21). The Lord Jesus said that unless we are born anew we cannot enter into the kingdom of God (John 3:5; cf. Titus 3:5). We all have been born again and can enter into the kingdom. Furthermore, by becoming pearls, we even become the entrance itself. (*Life-study of Genesis,* pp. 154-155)

Today's Reading

After entering the New Jerusalem through the gate of pearl, we find ourselves on the street of gold (Rev. 21:21). This means that we walk according to the divine nature and that the divine nature becomes our way. Regeneration is our gate; the divine nature is our way. Do not go to others to ask them what you should do. The Lord Jesus is your way (John 14:6). You simply need to walk according to the golden street, the divine nature within you. Brothers, do you get your haircut according to the divine nature?

Sisters, do you shop according to the divine nature?…To be on the street of gold is to touch the divine nature of God.

Although we may have the gate of pearl and the street of gold, we do not yet have a wall built up to express the image of God. The wall of the New Jerusalem is not only an erected boundary that separates the holy from the common, but also a building that expresses the image of God. In Revelation 4:2-3, God sitting on the throne has the appearance of jasper. The wall of the New Jerusalem and the first foundation stone of the wall are also built with jasper (Rev. 21:18-19), bearing the same appearance as God. Although we have passed through the gate of pearl and are walking the golden way, I still expect to see around us a wall built up to include all godly things, to exclude all worldly things, and to express the image of God. This wall is built up by the way of transformation (2 Cor. 3:18; Rom. 12:2a; 1 Cor. 3:12a). The materials of the wall are all transformed precious stones (Rev. 21:11, 18a, 19-20). Only transformed people can be built together.

A precious stone is a transformed item. All precious stones originally were of other materials. Some of them were formed into igneous rocks by pressure and heat. Others were formed into sedimentary rocks by pressure and by the flowing of water. All became precious stones.…Under extreme pressure and intense heat the carbon becomes a diamond. These are the principles of the transformation of precious stones. Oh, we need the burning, we need the flowing of the living water, and we need the pressure!

We were made earthen vessels. Although these vessels are useful, their material, which is clay, does not match the New Jerusalem. In the New Jerusalem there are no bricks, only transformed stones. We need a great amount of pressure and burning and flowing of life before we can be transformed into precious stones. The more pressure, burning, and flowing we experience, the more precious we become. (*Life-study of Genesis*, pp. 155-157)

Further Reading: The Application of the Interpretation of the New Jerusalem to the Seeking Believers, chs. 2-3

Enlightenment and inspiration: _____

_____

_____

_____

Morning Nourishment

1 Cor. For we are God's fellow workers; you are God's culti-
3:9 vated land, God's building.
    12 But if anyone builds upon the foundation gold, silver,
    precious stones...

In 1 Corinthians 3 Paul covers the matters of feeding, drinking, eating, planting, watering, and growing. These are all related to life. In 3:9 Paul goes on to refer to the church as God's farm and God's building. The farm certainly is a matter of life, and the building is the issue of life. No material building involves anything of life. But the spiritual building mentioned in this chapter has much to do with life. Paul talks about this building not only in 1 Corinthians, but also in Ephesians, Colossians, and Romans. However, the basic points regarding the building are covered in 1 Corinthians. God's building is altogether a building in life and of life, for it is the building up of the Body of Christ. (*Life-study of 1 Corinthians,* p. 271)

Today's Reading

Apparently, there is no connection between the farm and the building. According to our natural concept, a farm is a matter of life, but a building is a composition of lifeless materials. Thus, there does not seem to be a proper continuation between the expressions God's farm and God's building. However, if we realize that the building here is a life building, a building in life, we shall see that there is a direct connection, an excellent continuation, between the farm and the building. Whatever is produced on the farm is not for the farm itself; it is for the building. The produce grown on the farm is for the building.

Although the produce grown on the farm is for the building, it does not go into the building directly. Rather, we may say that it goes to the church restaurant to be eaten, digested, and assimilated by the saints. Through this process, what is grown on the farm is consumed by the saints and eventually even becomes them.

In order for the food we eat to become our constitution, there must be the process of metabolism. In the Bible this process is called transformation. Transformation involves a metabolic change. Hence, transformation is altogether a metabolic process. First we eat a meal. After a period of time, the food is digested and assimilated. Eventually, the digested and assimilated food becomes the fibers of our being. This is metabolism, transformation.

In order for an infant of seven pounds to grow into a mature man weighing one hundred seventy pounds, there must be a regular eating and a normal process of metabolism. Gradually, the food taken in by an infant will cause him to grow. Eventually, as a result of a metabolic process over a long period of time, he will become a full-grown man. As a mature man, he is a product, a composition, of all the food he has eaten, digested, and assimilated. This illustrates the process of spiritual metabolism. The produce grown on the farm is eaten and digested by us. Eventually, through the process of metabolism, this food supply becomes us and transforms us into material for the building up of the Body of Christ.

The church is a farm to grow Christ. Every item of the produce grown on the farm is Christ. The farm produce includes many different aspects of Christ. Christ is the milk, the vegetables, and the meat. The church grows Christ, and all the saints eat Christ. Eventually, through digestion, assimilation, and metabolism, Christ becomes us, and we become Him. Then we are the proper materials for the building.

Paul's writing in 1 Corinthians 3 has a direct connection from item to item. First he refers to feeding, drinking, and eating. Then he goes on to mention planting and watering, after which he tells us that it is God alone who gives the growth. Following this, he says in verse 9 that we are the farm and the building. Therefore, there is a direct connection between all these matters. As we have seen, the farm becomes the building. (*Life-study of 1 Corinthians*, pp. 271-273)

Further Reading: Life-study of 1 Corinthians, msg. 31

Enlightenment and inspiration: _____

_____

_____

Morning Nourishment

1 Cor. But if anyone builds upon the foundation gold, silver,
3:12-13 precious stones, wood, grass, stubble, the work of
each will become manifest; for the day will declare *it*,
because it is revealed by fire, and the fire itself will
prove each one's work, of what sort it is.
1 Pet. For "all flesh is like grass, and all its glory like
1:24 the flower of grass. The grass has withered, and the
flower has fallen off."

Paul warned us to build the church in a proper way. Most of the work among Christians is not with gold, silver or pearl, and precious stone, but with wood, grass, and stubble. As gold in typology signifies the divine nature, wood represents our human nature. Thus, wood is versus gold. We are fond of saying that we are all human, especially when we make a mistake. However, we should not make our humanity an excuse. Our humanity must be a resurrected humanity, for the natural humanity is inadequate for the building of God's church. The building of the church requires a transformed humanity, not a humanity of wood.

Grass is versus silver. The Bible tells us that all flesh is grass (Isa. 40:6; 1 Pet. 1:24). Grass typifies the people having become flesh. Grass is not solid like wood; it is weak and fragile. Thus, grass represents the fallen nature of man. (*Life-study of Genesis*, p. 157)

Today's Reading

The last item that Paul mentions in 1 Corinthians 3:12 is stubble. Stubble is the stock or stem of a crop which remains after the grain has been threshed. Stubble, which comes out of the ground, is versus the precious stone, which is a transformed substance. First Corinthians 3:12 presents a vivid contrast. Wood is a tree without fruit, and stubble is a crop without grain. We should not be wood or stubble, materials that will be burned away and that are useless for the building of God's church.

For the Lord's building, we need the divine gold, the regenerated pearl, and the transformed precious stones. The more we have of these items, the easier it will be for us to be built together spontaneously. If we experience the gold, pearl, and precious stones, we will not only be the precious materials, but also a building fitly joined together to form a habitation of God in our spirit (Eph. 2:22). Thus, transformation is for God's building. We need to pray about these matters and fellowship concerning them that the Lord may bring us all into the reality of transformation for His building. (*Life-study of Genesis*, pp. 157-158)

In 1 Corinthians 3:12 Paul refers to two ways of building....The first way is to build with gold, silver, and precious stones; the second way is to build with wood, grass, and stubble. Here we have two categories of building materials. Gold, silver, and precious stones are minerals. Wood, grass, and stubble are related to the plant life. We in the Lord's recovery all are doing the work of building. Thus, we must take heed how we build. Are we building with gold, silver, and precious stones, or with wood, grass, and stubble?

Paul's word in 3:12 is not only for elders or co-workers. On the contrary, it is written to every believer. This is included in an Epistle addressed to the church in Corinth, with all those who call upon the name of the Lord Jesus Christ in every place. Thus, this verse is intended for all of us. It applies to you and also to me.

In the building of the church we ourselves are used as material....[Hence], we need to ask what kind of material we are. Are we wood or gold, silver or grass, precious stones or stubble?...We are in the process of transformation. Therefore, in a sense we are both wood and gold, grass and silver, stubble and precious stones. Using an example from the insect world, we may compare ourselves to a caterpillar in a cocoon in the process of becoming a butterfly. On the one hand, we are still a caterpillar; on the other hand, there are signs that we are becoming a butterfly. The process of transformation has begun, but it is not yet complete. We are all on the way of transformation; we are in the process of being transformed. (*Life-study of 1 Corinthians*, p. 275)

Further Reading: Life-study of 1 Corinthians, msg. 31; Crystallization-study of Song of Songs, msg. 4

Enlightenment and inspiration: _____

_____

_____

Hymns, #837

1   We praise Thee, Lord, for Thy great plan
     That we Thy dwelling-place may be;
     Thou live in us, we filled with Thee,
     Thou in the Son expressed might be.

2   Though in Thine image made by Thee
     And given Thine authority,
     Yet we are only made of clay
     Without a trace of divinity.

3   When we receive Thee as our life,
     Thy nature we thru grace possess;
     Mingled together, we with Thee
     One Body glorious will express.

4   When flows Thy life thru all our souls,
     Filling, renewing every part,
     We will be pearls and precious stones,
     Changed to Thine image, as Thou art.

5   But, Lord, we fully realize
     These are not wrought men's praise to rouse,
     But as material to be built
     Together for Thy glorious house.

6   Here, Lord, we give ourselves to Thee;
     Receive us into Thy wise hands;
     Bend, break, and build together in Thee
     To be the house to meet Thy demands.

7   Break all the natural life for us,
     Deal Thou with each peculiar way,
     That we no more independent be
     But with all saints are one for aye.

8   Then we shall be Thy Bride beloved,
     Together in Thy chamber abide,
     Enjoy the fulness of Thy love.
     How Thou wilt then be satisfied!

Composition for prophecy with main point and sub-points: _____

The Work of the Divine Building

Scripture Reading: Eph. 2:21-22; 3:17a; 1 Cor. 3:6-17

Day 1 I. The work of the divine building is carried out through renewing and transformation (Rom. 12:2; 2 Cor. 3:18; 4:16; Eph. 4:23; Titus 3:5):

A. We need to be renewed and transformed, and then we can do the work of building (Rom. 12:2; Eph. 4:23, 12, 16):

1. To be renewed is to have God's element added into our being to replace and discharge our old element (2 Cor. 4:16; Titus 3:5).

2. The renewing Spirit is mingled with our regenerated spirit as one mingled spirit to spread into our mind to renew our entire being (Eph. 4:23).

3. In renewing, we are transferred from the realm of the old creation to the realm of the new creation to be the new man to fulfill God's eternal purpose (2 Cor. 5:17; Eph. 4:24; Col. 3:10).

4. Transformation is the metabolic function of the life of God in us, by the addition of the element of the divine life into our being, so that we may express the image of Christ outwardly (2 Cor. 3:18).

5. Transformation is for the mass reproduction of the firstborn Son of God as the prototype of a God-man so that we may be shaped in the divine image to be exactly like the firstborn Son of God (Rom. 8:29; Heb. 2:10).

B. Renewing issues in transformation, and transformation issues in building up; the building up of the jasper wall of the New Jerusalem goes along with transformation (Rom. 12:2; Rev. 21:18a).

Day 2 **II.** **The work of the divine building is the believ-**
    &   **ers' growth in the divine life and their being**
Day 3   **joined together in the divine life (Eph.**
       4:15-16; 2:21):

    A. When we grow in the divine life and when we
       are joined together in the divine life, we are in
       the building (v. 21).

    B. The building of the church as the house of God is
       by the believers' growth in life; the growth in life
       is the building (1 Cor. 3:6-9, 16-17; Eph.
       4:15-16).

    C. The boards of the tabernacle typify the believers
       joined together to be the dwelling place of God;
       the bars signify the initial Spirit becoming the
       uniting Spirit, who joins all the members of
       Christ into one Body (Exo. 26:15, 26-29; Eph.
       2:21-22; 4:3-4):

       1. In the uniting Spirit there is not only the
          divine element but also the human ele-
          ment; here we have both divinity (the one-
          ness of the Spirit) and humanity (the
          keeping of the oneness) (Exo. 26:26a, 29b;
          Eph. 4:2-3).

       2. The uniting bars signify not the Holy Spirit
          alone but the Holy Spirit mingled with the
          human spirit (1 Cor. 6:17; Rom. 8:4).

       3. The uniting bars are the mingled spirit, the
          divine Spirit mingled with the human
          spirit to become the uniting bond of peace
          (Eph. 4:3).

    D. The members of the Body are fitted together
       by holding the Head; there are no direct rela-
       tionships among the members in the Body,
       for all relationships are indirect, that is,
       through the Head and under the Head (Col.
       1:18; 2:19).

Day 4 **III.** **The work of the divine building is the believ-**
    ers' being built together in Christ into a
    dwelling place of God by the Spirit in their

spirit possessed by Christ, both of which are mingled as one spirit (Eph. 2:22; 1 Cor. 6:17):

A. Ephesians is a book on the Body, and every chapter contains a verse concerning the human spirit; this indicates that the Body is absolutely a matter in our regenerated spirit (1:22-23, 17; 2:22; 3:5, 16; 4:23; 5:18; 6:18).

B. Our spirit, as today's Jerusalem—the place where the God of our spirit dwells—is universally spacious, including not only our individual spirit but the spirits of all the saints (Rom. 8:16; Num. 16:22; Heb. 12:9; Eph. 2:22).

IV. The building is by the Spirit's operation, distributing to each member different gifts for the building up of the Body (1 Cor. 12:4, 7-11):

A. The Triune God moves in the believers for the accomplishing of His eternal purpose to build up the church, the Body of Christ, for the expression of God (vv. 4-6).

B. The manifestation of the Spirit is "for what is profitable," that is, for the growth in life of the members of the Body of Christ and for the building up of the Body (v. 7).

Day 5 V. The building work with gold, silver, and precious stones will be rewarded by Christ at His coming back (3:12-17):

A. The central work of God is to work Himself in Christ into our being, making Himself one with us and making us one with Him (Gal. 1:15-16a; 2:20; 4:19; Eph. 3:16-17a):

1. The intrinsic element of the work of the divine building is to minister the building and builded God into others for the building up of the Body of Christ (Matt. 16:18; Eph. 3:17a; 4:4, 12, 16).

2. The unique work of the ministry is to carry out God's economy to build Himself into man for the building up of the Body of

Day 6

Christ, consummating in the New Jerusalem (3:9-11; 4:11-12; Rev. 21:2).

B. A work to which God can fully commit Himself has four essential features (1 Cor. 15:58; 16:10):

1. There must be a revelation of the eternal purpose of God (Eph. 3:11).

2. The source and initiation of the work must be of God and not of ourselves (Matt. 15:13; 1 Cor. 8:6):

   a. God is the Father, and everything proceeds from Him (Rom. 11:36).

   b. In our work we must avoid the sin of presumption—the sin of acting outside of God to do what He has not commanded and to begin a work that He has not instructed us to do (Psa. 19:13; Num. 18:1-7).

3. The continuance and advance of God's work must be by God's power and not our power (2 Cor. 3:5; Phil. 3:10).

4. The result of God's work is for God's glory and not for our glory (John 7:17-18; 8:50; 12:43; Eph. 3:21).

C. If our work in building up the church is by our natural man (wood), by our fallen, fleshly man (grass), or by anything that issues from an earthen source (stubble), our work will be burned (1 Cor. 3:12-13, 15).

D. We all need to consider how we are building the church; we should be those who are building with the Divine Trinity as the precious and transformed materials (vv. 8, 10, 12-13).

Morning Nourishment

Eph. That you put off...the old man,...and *that* you be
4:22-23 renewed in the spirit of your mind.

Rom. And do not be fashioned according to this age, but be
12:2 transformed by the renewing of the mind that you
may prove what the will of God is, that which is good
and well pleasing and perfect.

2 Cor. But we all with unveiled face, beholding and reflect-
3:18 ing like a mirror the glory of the Lord, are being
transformed into the same image from glory to glory,
even as from the Lord Spirit.

In God's organic salvation we, the believers in Christ, can participate in God's divinity. God's life has been imparted into our life,
His nature is being wrought into our nature, His mind is being
wrought into our mind, and we even have His divine element,
the element of the riches of His unsearchable life, to transform
our entire being. Thus, we have God's life, God's nature, God's
mind, and the divine element of all His riches, and now we can
participate in God's divinity in full. For us to participate in God's
divinity means that He is making us Him. He is making us God
in His life, in His nature, in His thinking, and in His expression
but not, of course, in His Godhead. (*The Secret of God's Organic
Salvation, "The Spirit Himself with Our Spirit,"* p. 42)

Today's Reading

Transformation transforms the believers' entire being, by
the transforming Spirit in their spirit filled with Christ, into the
glorious image of Christ, that they may fully participate in God's
divinity. To be filled with Christ, who is divine, is to be filled with
divinity. At present we are participating in God's divinity only
partially, but when our entire being is transformed and filled
with divinity, we will fully participate in God's divinity.

Transformation is by renewing; it is the issue of renewing.
Romans 12:2 says, "Do not be fashioned according to this age,
but be transformed by the renewing of the mind." This indicates
that transformation is the issue of renewing....Renewing is

mainly in the believers' mind (Eph. 4:23); transformation is in the believers' soul for their entire being....Transformation is not any kind of outward correction or adjustment.

Transformation is a kind of metabolism, by the addition of the element of the divine life of Christ into the believers' being, to be expressed outwardly in the image of Christ. This can be illustrated by having a healthy complexion through proper nutrition. The way to have such a healthy complexion is not to apply cosmetics but to eat nourishing food and then to digest and assimilate it metabolically. If we eat properly, the food we digest and assimilate will supply us with a new element which will eventually produce an outward and visible change in our facial color. The principle is the same with transformation. Transformation is a matter of inward metabolism issuing in an outward expression.

Transformation is accomplished by the Lord Spirit (the pneumatic Christ), transforming the believers into the image of the glory of Christ (2 Cor. 3:18). The metabolism involved in transformation eventually transforms us into the image of the glory of Christ.

Transformation should be consummated by conformation, which is maturity in the divine life for the believers to be conformed to the image of Christ, the firstborn Son of God, to fully participate in God's divinity. Thus, they manifest God in life, in nature, in inward thinking, and in outward expression to enjoy the divine sonship and to participate in God's divinity in full.

For God to work Himself into us in such a way is not merely to make us holy, and it is not merely to make us perfect, victorious, and spiritual. God is working His life, nature, mind, and element into us in order to make us God in life, in nature, in mind, and in expression. (*The Secret of God's Organic Salvation*, "The Spirit Himself with Our Spirit," pp. 40-42)

Further Reading: The Secret of God's Organic Salvation, "The Spirit Himself with Our Spirit," chs. 3-4

Enlightenment and inspiration: _____

_____

_____

_____

Morning Nourishment

Exo. And you shall make the boards for the tabernacle of
26:15 acacia wood, standing up.

26-29 And you shall make bars of acacia wood....And the middle bar shall pass through in the center of the boards from end to end. And you shall overlay the boards with gold, and make their rings of gold as holders for the bars; and you shall overlay the bars with gold.

Eph. With all lowliness and meekness, with long-suffering,
4:2-3 bearing one another in love, being diligent to keep the oneness of the Spirit in the uniting bond of peace.

The building of the tabernacle in Exodus corresponds to the oneness in John 17. The Lord prayed that all His believers would be one so that God could have a dwelling place on earth. The tabernacle was such a dwelling place.

[The oneness depicted by the tabernacle] has three aspects. The first aspect, the initial aspect, is with the golden rings. I am quite certain that the golden rings were attached to the boards before the boards were overlaid with gold. Thus, the first step was to attach the rings to the boards, and the second step was to overlay the boards with gold. The third step was to make the uniting bars, which held the forty-eight boards together and brought them into oneness. This oneness is the building, which is the dwelling place of God....By considering the picture of the tabernacle, we can have the proper understanding of the practical oneness for which the Lord Jesus prayed [in John 17]. (*Truth Messages*, pp. 101-102)

Today's Reading

This oneness is in the Triune God. The boards were one in the gold, and the gold signifies the nature of God....On each board there were the three rings signifying the Triune God....This is the initial Spirit, the sealing Spirit, we have received as the rings.

After we are regenerated, the sealing Spirit begins to spread throughout our being,...overlaying us with gold.

Although we may have the initial Spirit and some experience of being overlaid with gold, we still need to go on to the uniting

Spirit. After the boards, the rings, and the overlaying gold, we still need the bars. Without the bars, the forty-eight boards cannot be one, for it is the bars that hold them together....We are the boards, ...the rings signify the Triune God, and the gold covering the boards signifies the spreading of God. Just as the rings are a symbol of the initial Spirit, the bars are a symbol of the uniting Spirit. The boards stand upright, and the bars unite them by crossing them horizontally.

For us, the standing boards, to have acacia wood overlaid with gold is quite understandable. But what does it mean to say that the uniting Spirit has humanity, typified by acacia wood, overlaid with divinity, typified by gold?

Ephesians 4:2 and 3 help us to understand this matter. Verse 3 speaks of being diligent to keep the oneness of the Spirit in the uniting bond of peace. Although the oneness is the oneness of the Spirit, it is a oneness we must keep. The keeping of the oneness is our responsibility, not the responsibility of the Spirit. Here we have both divinity, the oneness of the Spirit, and humanity, the keeping of the oneness. If we have the oneness of the Spirit without the keeping of the oneness, we shall be short. Therefore, we need to be diligent to keep the oneness. The keeping of the oneness spoken of in verse 3 is related to the virtues mentioned in verse 2. We must keep the oneness of the Spirit by having lowliness, meekness, and long-suffering and by bearing one another in love,...[which] are all human virtues signified by the acacia wood within the uniting bars. Therefore, in order to keep the oneness of the Spirit, we need a humanity with certain virtues.

The uniting bars are not the Holy Spirit alone, but the Holy Spirit with the human spirit....It denotes the mingled spirit.... The Spirit represented by these bars also includes the human spirit. This means that if our spirit does not cooperate with the uniting Spirit, the oneness cannot be realized in a practical way. (*Truth Messages,* pp. 102-106)

Further Reading: Truth Messages, chs. 10-11

Enlightenment and inspiration: _____

_____

_____

Morning Nourishment

John   That they all may be one; even as You, Father, are in
17:21-23 Me and I in You, that they also may be in Us....That
          they may be one, even as We are one; I in them, and
          You in Me, that they may be perfected into one...
Exo.   And you shall make the boards for the tabernacle of
26:15   acacia wood, standing up.
28   And the middle bar shall pass through in the center
          of the boards from end to end.
Eph.   In whom all the building, being fitted together, is
2:21-22   growing into a holy temple in the Lord; in whom you
          also are being built together into a dwelling place of
          God in spirit.

In order for the uniting Spirit to pass through us and thus join us with others, we need to receive the cross, for the uniting Spirit always crosses the standing boards. If we are willing to receive the cross, our spirit will cooperate with the uniting Spirit. Then the Spirit with our spirit will join us to another believer in Christ....We stand, but we are crossed by the Spirit....This is the unique way to keep the oneness.

There are several steps to the oneness portrayed in the tabernacle. First, we have the initial Spirit, who is the regenerating and sealing Spirit. Then we have the process of transformation by which we are transformed into acacia wood. Along with transformation, there is the overlaying of the wood with the divine nature. Furthermore, the Spirit is continually endeavoring to cross us, to pass through us. In order for this to take place, our spirit, with our mind, will, and emotion, must go along with Him. Only then do we have the uniting bars, the five bars in three rows to unite the believers into one. When we have all these aspects, we have the oneness in the Triune God revealed in John 17. This means we have the building in the overlaying and uniting gold. (*Truth Messages*, pp. 106-107)

Today's Reading

We need to emphasize the importance of being crossed by the uniting Spirit....If we are willing to be crossed, it means that our spirit goes along with the crossing Spirit. The Spirit will never join us to others without this willingness. The uniting Spirit cannot unite me to you unless your spirit is willing to cooperate with the Spirit. When the uniting Spirit comes to me, it comes with the spirit of another brother, and when it goes from me to still another, it goes with my spirit. The uniting Spirit cannot unite us Himself. He must have the cooperation of our spirit. This means that we must be willing to be crossed by Him.

If we see this matter, then we shall realize why, even after more than nineteen centuries, the oneness for which the Lord prayed in John 17 has not yet come into existence. Among today's Christians there is little transformation or overlaying with the divine nature. Furthermore, there is little crossing of the Spirit and little cooperation of the human spirit with the divine Spirit. Hence, there is no oneness. But what about the situation among us in the Lord's recovery?…Yes, you may be standing firmly for the Lord's testimony as one of the boards, but are you willing to be crossed by the Spirit?…Is your spirit willing to go with the Spirit to another saint? Please do not think that the Spirit of God Himself alone can unite us. No, He needs our spirit to go along with Him. This is the meaning of keeping the oneness of the Spirit with all lowliness, meekness, long-suffering, and with bearing one another in love.

If you have this willingness, you will immediately and spontaneously have the uniting bars, and you will experience the practical oneness. The Holy Spirit with your spirit will pass on to the spirit of another saint. This will in turn help other brothers and sisters to be willing for the uniting Spirit to cross them.

The uniting Spirit crosses through all the members of the Body when the spirits of the members are willing to be crossed by Him. Through this willingness and this crossing we have the oneness. It was in this way that the entire tabernacle was brought into one. This is the oneness for the building, the dwelling place of God. (*Truth Messages*, pp. 107-109)

Further Reading: Life-study of Exodus, msgs. 97-98

Enlightenment and inspiration: _____

_____

_____

_____

Morning Nourishment

Eph. In whom all the building, being fitted together, is
2:21-22 growing into a holy temple in the Lord; in whom you
also are being built together into a dwelling place of
God in spirit.
4:15-16 But holding to truth in love, we may grow up into
Him in all things, who is the Head, Christ, out from
whom all the Body, being joined together and being
knit together,...causes the growth of the Body unto
the building up of itself in love.
1 Cor. But if anyone builds upon the foundation gold, silver,
3:12-13 precious stones, wood, grass, stubble, the work of
each will become manifest; for the day will declare *it*,
because it is revealed by fire, and the fire itself will
prove each one's work, of what sort it is.

God's habitation, His dwelling place, is in our spirit (Eph.
2:22). In type, the ancient city of Jerusalem was God's dwelling
place, but today God's dwelling place is in our spirit. Our regenerated spirit is today's Jerusalem. You may think that there is no
comparison between the city of Jerusalem and our spirit. Jerusalem was a large city, and our spirit is very small. But if you know
the Bible, you will realize that our spirit today is much larger
than Jerusalem. Our spirit is universally spacious. The problem
is that we are too individualistic and think only of our individual
spirit. But when the Bible speaks of "your spirit," it includes the
spirits of all the saints. (*Life-study of Ephesians,* pp. 212-213)

Today's Reading

For too long our mind has been preoccupied by natural concepts, religious thoughts, and traditional teachings. In considering the matter of our spirit, we need to drop all this and see that
our spirit is universally spacious. We know that God dwells in
the third heaven, but He also dwells in our spirit. This makes
our spirit today's Jerusalem. Hallelujah for that wonderful entity
in the universe called our spirit! The Spirit witnesses with our
spirit (Rom. 8:16). The words "our spirit" include Paul's spirit,

Martin Luther's spirit, John Wesley's spirit, Brother Nee's spirit, your spirit, and my spirit. How spacious our spirit is! The Bible reveals that God is the God of our spirit (Num. 16:22; Heb. 12:9). Where is God today? In our spirit. Where is God's dwelling place today? In our spirit. (*Life-study of Ephesians,* p. 213)

The work of the divine building is the believers' growth in the divine life and their being joined together in the divine life (Eph. 4:15-16; 2:21)....The actual building is our growth and our union in the divine life. When we grow in the divine life and when we are joined together in the divine life, we are in the building.

The work of the divine building is also the believers' being built together in Christ into a dwelling of God by the Spirit in their spirit possessed by Christ, both of which are mingled as one spirit (Eph. 2:22).

The building is also by the Spirit's operation, distributing to each member different gifts for the building up of the Body (1 Cor. 12:4, 7-11). The Spirit's distributing different gifts to different members is the actual building work.

The building work with gold, silver, and precious stones will be rewarded by Christ at His coming back. However, if the work is with wood, grass, and stubble, it will be burned on the day of the Lord's coming (1 Cor. 3:12-14).

If we build the church with God the Father as gold, with God the Son as silver, and with God the Spirit as precious stones, we will receive the reward. However, if we do the work of the building by the natural man, by the fallen man, and with things that issue from the earthen source, our work will be burned, yet we ourselves will be saved. We all need to consider how we are building the church. We should be those who are building with the Divine Trinity as the precious and transformed materials. (*The Secret of God's Organic Salvation,* "*The Spirit Himself with Our Spirit,*" pp. 59-60)

Further Reading: Life-study of Ephesians, msg. 24; Elders' Training, Book 7: One Accord for the Lord's Move, ch. 7

Enlightenment and inspiration: _____

_____

_____

_____

Morning Nourishment

1 Cor. The work of each will become manifest,...because it is
3:13-17 revealed by fire, and the fire itself will prove each one's
work, of what sort it is. If anyone's work which he has
built upon *the foundation* remains, he will receive a
reward; if anyone's work is consumed, he will suffer
loss....Do you not know that you are the temple of God,
and *that* the Spirit of God dwells in you? If anyone
destroys the temple of God, God will destroy him...

First Corinthians 3 shows us what life is. First, we all have to
realize that we are plants....Let us forget about things such as service, work, eldership, and apostleship....I am a little plant. As a
little plant in life, I need to grow, and to grow I need water. I will
take water from whoever can water me. Then I will grow. Furthermore, I want to be transformed into precious material for God's
building—gold, silver, and precious stone. The first basic thing we
have to learn is the matter of the growth in life. As a plant I am
growing in the soil with all the riches. My soil is the processed and
consummated Triune God. I want to dwell in Him and be rooted
down in Him to absorb all His riches through my contacting Him.
...Then I will grow into transformation to become precious material for His unique building in this universe. While I am growing,
He will lead me to participate in the divine work. (*Elders' Training,
Book 7: One Accord for the Lord's Move,* pp. 91-92)

Today's Reading

I work in this divine building, not by my natural ability, not by
wood, grass, or stubble. These categories of material are natural and
worldly, having nothing to do with growth, life, and transformation.
I would never work with this kind of material. I should deny myself,
put my soul life aside, and condemn my natural ability....I build
with my growth, with my enjoyment of the Triune God. This is
what it means to build with gold, silver, and precious stones.

I am also careful not to damage or destroy Christ's Body; otherwise, I will suffer destruction because the church, Christ's Body
and God's temple, is a treasure so dear and precious to Him,

purchased with His own blood (Acts 20:28)....I do not want to be a Christian like the Corinthians. They did not take care of the growth in life....They were still babes...(1 Cor. 3:1-3). Because they were fleshly and even fleshy, Paul could not give them solid food. He could only feed them with milk. (*Elders' Training, Book 7: One Accord for the Lord's Move*, p. 92)

Our work in the recovery today is to minister God to people. Yes, we need to save sinners and to feed the saints and perfect them. The crucial matter, however, is that we minister God to others. The God whom we minister is not just the building God—He is also the builded God. If we fail to minister God in this way, our work will be wood, grass, and stubble (1 Cor. 3:12).

I would ask you to reconsider the work you are doing for the Lord. Perhaps you have opened up a region or have brought many people to God. But...how much of Christ as the embodiment of the Triune God has been wrought into those whom you have brought to God? If we are sincere and genuine, we will humble ourselves and confess that not very much of the Triune God has been wrought into the ones we have brought to God. Therefore, we need to practice one thing—to minister the processed Triune God into others so that He may build Himself into their inner man. In every aspect of our work—preaching the gospel, feeding the believers, perfecting the saints—the intrinsic element must be that we minister the building and builded God to others. I would urge you to pray that the Lord would teach you to work in this way.

The processed Triune God is embodied in Christ and realized as the consummated Spirit. This is the God whom we worship, preach, and minister to others. Today He is building Himself into His redeemed people in order to produce a house with Himself as the element and also with something from their redeemed and uplifted humanity. This house is the church, the Body of Christ. This house is the enlargement, the expansion, of Christ, the embodiment of the Triune God realized as the Spirit. (Life-study of 1 & 2 Samuel, pp. 200-201)

Further Reading: Life-study of 1 & 2 Samuel, msgs. 29-31

Enlightenment and inspiration: _____

_____

_____

_____

Morning Nourishment

Eph. According to the eternal purpose which He made in
3:11 Christ Jesus our Lord.
Rom. Because out from Him and through Him and to Him
11:36 are all things. To Him be the glory forever. Amen.

[There are] four essential features of a work to which God can
fully commit Himself. The first vital need is of a true revelation to
our hearts of the eternal purpose of God. We cannot do without
this....Today evangelism is assumed by most Christians to be *the*
work of God. But evangelism can never be an unrelated thing. It
must be integrated with God's whole plan, for it is in fact but a
means to an end. That end is the preeminence of the Son of God,
and evangelism is bringing in the sons among whom He shall
stand preeminent. (*The Collected Works of Watchman Nee*, vol. 39,
"Sit, Walk, Stand," pp. 44-45)

Today's Reading

In Paul's generation every believer had a specific relation to the
eternal purpose of God (see especially Ephesians 4:11-16). That
should be no less true of us today. The eyes of God are turning
towards His coming kingdom....But as with the kingdom of Solomon, so now, there is first a period of spiritual warfare represented
by the reign of David. God is seeking those who will cooperate with
Him today in that preparatory warfare.

All Christian work that is not [identified with the eternal purpose of God] is fragmentary and unrelated, and it does not ultimately get anywhere. We have to seek from God a revelation to our
hearts by His Holy Spirit of "the counsel of his will" (see 1:9-12) and
then to ask ourselves...: "Is [our work] directly related to that?"
When that is settled, all the small questions of daily guidance will
solve themselves.

Secondly, all work that is going to be effective in the divine purpose
must be conceived by God. If *we* plan work and then ask God to bless
it, we need not expect God to commit Himself to it. God's name can
never be a "rubber stamp" to authorize work that is ours in conception.

I must have, therefore, a knowledge of God's will in my

particular sphere of work. Out of that knowledge only should the work be initiated. The abiding principle of all true Christian work is: "In the beginning God…"

Thirdly, all work to be effective must depend for its continuance upon the power of God alone.…We say of a man, "He is a very powerful speaker," but we have to ask ourselves the question: What power is he using? Is it spiritual power or is it natural power? There is today all too much place given to the power of nature in the service of God. …Even where God has initiated a work, if we are trying to accomplish it in our own power God will never commit Himself to it.

When we come to an end of our works, His work begins. Thus the fire in the days to come and the Cross today effect the same thing. What cannot stand the Cross today will not survive the fire later. If *my* work, which is done in *my* power is brought to death, how much comes out of the grave? Nothing! Nothing ever survives the Cross but what is wholly of God in Christ.

God never asks us to do anything we *can* do. He asks us to live a life which we can never live and to do a work which we can never do. Yet, by His grace, we *are* living it and doing it. The life we live is the life of Christ lived in the power of God, and the work we do is the work of Christ carried on through us by His Spirit whom we obey. Self is the only obstruction to that life and to that work. May we each one pray from our hearts: "O Lord, deal with *me!*"

Finally, the end and object of all work to which God can commit Himself must be His glory. This means that we get nothing out of it for ourselves.…The less we get of personal gratification out of such a work the greater is its true value to God. There is no room for glory to man in the work of God. True, there is a deep, precious joy in any service that brings Him pleasure and that opens the door to His working, but the ground of that joy is His glory and not man's. Everything is "to the praise of the glory of his grace" (1:6, 12, 14). (*The Collected Works of Watchman Nee,* vol. 39, "Sit, Walk, Stand," pp. 45-48)

Further Reading: The Collected Works of Watchman Nee, vol. 9, pp. 287-304; vol. 39, "Sit, Walk, Stand," pp. 43-48; vol. 42, ch. 45

Enlightenment and inspiration: _____

_____

_____

_____

Hymns, #840

1 Freed from self and Adam's nature,
    Lord, I would be built by Thee
With the saints into Thy temple,
    Where Thy glory we shall see.
From peculiar traits deliver,
    From my independent ways,
That a dwelling place for Thee, Lord,
    We will be thru all our days.

2 By Thy life and by its flowing
    I can grow and be transformed,
With the saints coordinated,
    Builded up, to Thee conformed;
Keep the order in the Body,
    There to function in Thy will,
Ever serving, helping others,
    All Thy purpose to fulfill.

3 In my knowledge and experience
    I would not exalted be,
But submitting and accepting
    Let the Body balance me;
Holding fast the Head, and growing
    With His increase, in His way,
By the joints and bands supplying,
    Knit together day by day.

4 By Thy Spirit daily strengthened
    In the inner man with might,
I would know Thy love surpassing,
    Know Thy breadth and length and height;
Ever of Thy riches taking,
    Unto all Thy fulness filled,
Ever growing into manhood,
    That Thy Body Thou may build.

5 In God's house and in Thy Body
    Builded up I long to be,
That within this corporate vessel
    All shall then Thy glory see;
That Thy Bride, the glorious city,
    May appear upon the earth,
As a lampstand brightly beaming
    To express to all Thy worth.

Composition for prophecy with main point and sub-points: _____

_____

_____

_____

_____

_____

_____

_____

_____

_____

_____

_____

_____

_____

_____

_____

_____

_____

_____

_____

_____

_____

_____

_____

_____

_____

_____

_____

_____

_____

_____

_____

_____

The Accomplishment of the Divine Building

Scripture Reading: 1 Tim. 3:15; 1 Cor. 3:16-17; Eph. 1:22-23; 2:21-22; 4:12, 16

Day 1   I. The accomplishment of the divine building is the church in many localities as the house of God to be God's dwelling place, the holy temple in the Lord (1 Tim. 3:15; Eph. 2:21-22; 1 Cor. 1:2; 3:16-17):

A. The divine building has both a universal aspect and a local aspect (Eph. 2:21-22):

1. The phrase *all the building* in Ephesians 2:21 denotes the universal building, the building of the church throughout the universe:

   a. In Christ all the building is fitted together and is growing into a holy temple in the Lord.

   b. Since the building is living (1 Pet. 2:5), it is growing; the actual building of the church as the house of God is by the believers' growth in life (Eph. 4:15-16).

   c. In speaking of the universal building, we must distinguish such building from organization; the churches will be built together universally, but they will not be universally organized (2:21).

2. The words *you also* in Ephesians 2:22 indicate that the building in verse 21 is universal, but the building in verse 22 is local:

   a. Universally, the church is uniquely one and is growing into a holy temple; locally, the church in a particular locality also is one, and the local saints are being built together into a dwelling place of God in their particular locality.

   b. Universal building can be accomplished only through local building (1 Cor. 14:4-5, 12).

Day 2   B. The building of God is not an ordinary building;
it is the sanctuary of the holy God, the temple in
which the Spirit of God dwells (3:16-17):

1. The unique spiritual temple of God in the
universe has its expression in many localities on earth; each expression is the temple
of God in that locality (1:2; 3:16).

2. The temple of God in verse 16 refers to the
believers collectively in a certain locality (1:2).

3. The temple of God in 3:17 refers to all the
believers universally (Eph. 2:21).

C. How much building we have universally and
locally depends on how much we realize that
Christ is everything in God's economy (Col.
3:10-11):

1. Christ is the all-inclusive One, and we
should not hold on to anything in place of
Him (1:18; 2:19; 1 Cor. 1:30; 3:11).

2. If we hold to Christ as everything to us, we
will experience the genuine building, first
locally and then universally (Eph. 3:8;
1:22-23; 2:21-22).

Day 3   II. **The accomplishment of the divine building
is the Body of Christ in the whole universe
as the expression of Christ (1:23):**

A. The Lord's recovery is for the building up of the
Body of Christ (4:16):

K   1. All the churches are one Body, and the
co-workers should be doing not a regional
work but a universal work for the universal
Body (vv. 11-12).

2. Whatever the co-workers and elders do
locally or universally should be done with
a full realization that they are building
up the Body of Christ; thus, they should
always keep a view of the Body (v. 16):

a. All the problems of the church today are
due to the ignorance concerning the Body
of Christ (1:17-23; 1 Cor. 12:24b-27).

b. Whenever we do something, we should
have a proper consideration for the Body
(Rom. 12:4-5, 15).
3. In fact, all the believers in Christ have been
baptized into one Body by the Spirit; in
practicality, all the believers must be built
together into the Body of Christ by the
builders of the divine building throughout
the age of the New Testament (1 Cor. 12:13;
Eph. 4:11-12).

Day 4 B. Our work is the work of the Lord's recovery for
the building up of the Body of Christ (1 Cor.
15:58; 16:10; Eph. 4:12):
1. The Body of Christ is organic, and it is not
built up through natural methods or human
work (vv. 15-16).
2. "Whenever God's children see the oneness
of the Body, they will also see the oneness of
the work, and they will be delivered out of
individualistic work into the work of the
Body" (*The Collected Works of Watchman
Nee*, vol. 37, p. 244).

Day 5 C. The Body is universally one; for this reason the
local churches should not be isolated from one
another (Col. 4:14-16; Rev. 1:11; 2:1, 7a; 22:16a):
1. Isolation is contrary to the truth concerning the oneness of the Body; because each
local church is part of the Body universally,
no church should be isolated from others
(1 Cor. 1:2; 12:12-13, 27; Eph. 4:4).
2. Because the Body is receiving a continual
transfusion, to be isolated is to be cut off
both from the transfusion and from the
circulation of life in the Body; such a thing
violates the law of the Body (1:22-23; 1 Cor.
10:16-17).

Day 6 D. The Body of Christ is the goal of God's economy,
and the local churches are the procedure that God
takes to accomplish the building up of the Body

of Christ (Matt. 16:18; 18:17; 1 Cor. 12:12-13; 1:2; Rom. 12:4-5; 16:1, 3-5, 16b):

1. We need to be in the local churches so that we can be ushered into the reality of the Body of Christ (1 Cor. 1:2; 12:12-13, 27).

2. We should pay more attention to the Body of Christ than to the local churches (Eph. 1:22-23; 2:21-22; 4:4, 12, 16).

3. In the Lord's recovery we are building up the local churches for the building up of the Body of Christ, which will consummate in the New Jerusalem (1 Cor. 14:4-5, 12; 12:27; Eph. 2:21-22; 4:16; Rev. 21:2).

4. For the building up of the Body of Christ, there should be as much blending of all the local churches as practicality allows, without boundaries of states or nations (1 Cor. 12:27).

E. The Lord Jesus has an urgent need for the Body to be expressed in the local churches; unless there is a substantial expression of the Body of Christ on earth, the Lord Jesus will not return (Matt. 16:18, 27; Eph. 5:23, 27; Rev. 19:7).

church =
1) universal
2) local

Morning Nourishment

Eph. In whom all the building, being fitted together, is
2:21-22 growing into a holy temple in the Lord; in whom
you also are being built together into a dwelling
place of God in spirit.

1 Cor. So also you, since you are zealous of spirits, seek
14:12 that you may excel for the building up of the
church.

Chapter two of Ephesians concludes with the matter of the
building. In verse 21 we see the universal building, and in verse 22,
the local building. [In verse 21]...the phrase "all the building"
denotes the universal building, the church throughout the universe. The words "in whom you also" in verse 22 denote the local
building, the building among those in the city to which this Epistle was sent. The building, therefore, has a universal aspect and a
local aspect. It is significant that this chapter of Ephesians concludes with the building of the church in these two aspects.

For centuries, this matter of the building has been neglected.
Very few servants of the Lord have given it adequate attention.
Beginning in 1938, among us the Lord began to emphasize the
importance of the building. (*Life-study of Ephesians,* p. 735)

Today's Reading

Although there are millions of Christians on earth today, very
few have been built up with others. The reason for this lack of
building is that so many believers still hold on to ordinances. Perhaps you were a member of a certain denomination. However,
because of your ordinances, you were not one with others, and you
were not able to be built up with them. Rather, you were waiting
for the situation to change to fit your ordinances. When there was
no change or improvement, you moved to another group....In our
experience Christ must be everything to us: our peace, our foundation, our cornerstone. We should not care for anything other
than Christ. Whether the meetings are noisy or quiet makes no
difference. We are not for noise or for silence—we are for Christ.
By caring only for Christ, we can easily be one with others and be

built up with them locally and universally on Christ as the unique foundation.

In 2:22 Paul speaks of the local building.…The word "you" refers to the local saints. Furthermore, the word "also" indicates that the building in verse 22 is local. According to the context, the dwelling place of God in this verse is local, whereas the holy temple in the preceding verse is universal.

Paul is careful to point out that it is in Christ that the local saints are built together into a dwelling place of God in spirit. They are not built in ordinances, in practices, or in opinions. We can be built up only in the all-inclusive Christ who is our peace, foundation, and cornerstone.

It is important to see that the universal building can be accomplished only through the local building. If we are not built up with others in our own locality, we should not expect to be able to be built up in any other locality. All those who are burdened to migrate for the spread of the church life must firstly be built up in their own locality. If you have not yet been built up in your local church, I encourage you not to migrate. Before we can be built up universally, we must be built up in a practical way locally.

Nothing tests your spiritual maturity as much as this matter of building. Furthermore, the local building is a great help in your spiritual growth. If you are willing to be built into the church in your locality, you will have the abundance of the growth in life. The building must begin with the local aspect and then spread to the universal aspect.…Instead of withdrawing or holding back, we should be willing to be broken and even "wrecked" in order to be built up with others. What a difference this makes to our growth in life! If we grow in this way, the church life will spread both through us and with us.…Only those who have been built up locally can support the spread of the church life through migration. (*Life-study of Ephesians*, pp. 737-741)

Further Reading: Life-study of Ephesians, msg. 88; *The Conclusion of the New Testament*, msgs. 199-200

Enlightenment and inspiration: _____
_____
_____
_____

Morning Nourishment

Col.   **And not holding the Head, out from whom all the**
2:19   **Body...grows with the growth of God.**

3:10-11 **And have put on the new man, which is being renewed**
unto full knowledge according to the image of Him
who created him, where there cannot be Greek and
Jew, circumcision and uncircumcision, barbarian,
Scythian, slave, free man, but Christ is all and in all.

The spread of the Lord's recovery is the move of the living
Christ in our spirit in a corporate way. The Lord's move is with the
saints not individualistically, but corporately. As those who seek
the Lord, we should not hold anything back from Him. On the
contrary, we should always give in to Him and be willing to be
broken so that we may be built into the church in our locality.
Then wherever we may be, the recovery of the Lord will spread
through us. This is altogether different from a movement of man
or an organization. For the genuine move of Christ as the life-
giving Spirit in His Body, we need the local building.

We thank the Lord for the many churches raised up through
migration. We also thank Him for the many who have been useful
in migration because they had experienced some amount of local
building before they migrated. (*Life-study of Ephesians*, p. 741)

Today's Reading

The success of migration depends on the degree of building. If
we are built up in an absolute way, migration will proceed also in
an absolute way. But if we compromise with the local building, we
shall also compromise in any future migration.

How much building we have universally as well as locally depends on how much we give up the ordinances and realize in a
practical way that Christ is everything in God's economy. Since
He is the all-inclusive One, we should not hold on to anything in
place of Him. If we hold to Christ as everything to us, we shall experience the genuine building, first locally and then universally.
This will make us useful in migration for the expansion of the
church life. (*Life-study of Ephesians*, p. 741)

Today the Lord has an urgent need on the earth. He needs the reality of the Body to be expressed in each locality....We are here for only one thing, that is, to be in spirit....To be in spirit is to be in Christ. Today the Lord needs this kind of testimony on the earth. In locality after locality, no matter how many people there are in the church life, all are one in spirit. "There cannot be Jew nor Greek, there cannot be slave nor free man, there cannot be male and female" (Gal. 3:28). Here there is only Christ. We all have become one in Christ. This is what the Lord wants today. This should not be the case only in one locality, but even when many localities come together, all are one....In Christ we are all one. The same is true not only among a few localities, but even when many countries are gathered together....This is the Body which the Lord wants. The Body is not only local but also universal. In principle it is one, whether in its local aspect or in its universal aspect.

Christ today is not a local Christ but a universal Christ, and this universal Christ has a part of Himself in every locality. The part in Taipei is called the church in Taipei,...and the part in New York is called the church in New York. Every local church is a part of Christ. All these parts constitute the Body.

What is the Body? The Body is the fullness of Christ. In doctrine the church is the Body, but as to reality there is still a question of how much element of the Body is there....We should not condemn others; we must see our own condition....We all must confess in the light of the Lord that even we ourselves up to this day may live only thirty percent by the Spirit, leaving seventy percent that we live by ourselves. Have you seen this? This is the Lord's need today. The Lord does not merely need a church in each locality; He needs a Body. As soon as we do not live by Christ, as soon as we are not living by the Spirit, we are not the Body. In name we are still the church, but in reality we are not the Body. Why? Because the Body is the fullness of Christ. (*One Body, One Spirit, and One New Man,* pp. 31-33, 35-36)

Further Reading: One Body, One Spirit, and One New Man, chs. 3-4

Enlightenment and inspiration: _____

_____

_____

_____

Morning Nourishment

Eph. That the God of our Lord Jesus Christ, the Father of
1:17 glory, may give to you a spirit of wisdom and revelation in the full knowledge of Him.
22-23 And He subjected all things under His feet and gave Him *to be* Head over all things to the church, which is His Body, the fullness of the One who fills all in all.
Rom. So we who are many are one Body in Christ, and in-
12:5 dividually members one of another.

The essential, crystallized significance of the Body of Christ is that the Triune God is constituted with His chosen and redeemed people to become a constitution, a constituted entity. Unless we see this,...there will be no way to carry out what we are trying to do in the church today. If we see this essential significance, there will be no problem whatever.

In the New Testament it is not a matter of the oneness of the church; oneness is not something of the church but of the Body. The Lord's prayer for the believers in John 17 was concerning the Body. He prayed, "Holy Father, keep them in Your name, which You have given to Me, that they may be one even as We are....That they all may be one; even as You, Father, are in Me and I in You, that they also may be in Us" (vv. 11b, 21). The believers can have this oneness only by being in the Holy Father, in the Holy Son, and in the Holy Trinity. (*The Governing and Controlling Vision in the Bible*, pp. 28-29)

Today's Reading

The oneness that the Lord aspired for and prayed for in John 17 corresponds with the oneness of the Spirit in Ephesians 4:3-6. We must see that the church is the Body of Christ, which is a constitution, an entity constituted with the Triune God and His chosen and redeemed ones. In this Body there is the reality of oneness. The genuine oneness is not of the church but of the Body; the real oneness is the organic oneness of the Body. In a locality, this oneness is called *one accord*. Without the oneness of the Body, there is no possibility to have one accord in the church.

Brother Nee truly knew Christ and the Body. His work was not for himself at all; he did not have his own work. He never put any church he established "in his pocket." Brother Nee was the pioneer, and I am a follower....Neither Brother Nee nor I carried out our own work; rather, we carried out the work of the Lord's recovery. The Lord's recovery is for the building of the Body of Christ.

I called several urgent meetings for the elders and co-workers since 1984...because I observed that among us there was an inclination toward division....I said that the age of feudalism is over and that we should no longer do the work of feudal princes. The co-workers should go out, but they should never do the work of building fortresses, the work of the feudal princes; they should only do the work of the Lord's recovery. If we all do the work of the Lord's recovery, there will be the one Body. If only three or five people who are of the same mind go out to work in a small region, the outcome is not oneness or one accord; rather, that outcome creates division. This is the very reason for the turmoil in recent years.

In the early days of the church in Taipei, we were subdivided into four to five halls. In a certain hall several people would be joined together in one accord to do their own work. Their one accord included only those who were joined to them and excluded all the other halls. As a result, their hall became a small fortress with themselves as feudal princes. If a local church does not care for other local churches, that is a fortress under a feudal prince. Anyone who does the work of the fortress and the feudal prince will not have a long-lasting spiritual life....We all must see the Body and do the work of the Body. All our problems...are due to our lack of seeing the Body.

We need to see that the Body of Christ is not the oneness in a locality but the oneness of the Body, the oneness of the Spirit. There are thousands of local churches, but the Spirit is one. In the Body we need to keep the oneness of the Spirit; in the church and among the churches we need to be in one accord. This is the genuine oneness. (*The Governing and Controlling Vision in the Bible*, pp. 29-34)

Further Reading: The Governing and Controlling Vision in the Bible, ch. 2; *The Problems Causing the Turmoils in the Church Life*, ch. 2

Enlightenment and inspiration: _____

_____

_____

Morning Nourishment

1 Cor. For even as the body is one and has many members,
12:12-13 yet all the members of the body, being many, are one
body, so also is the Christ. For also in one Spirit we
were all baptized into one Body, whether Jews or
Greeks, whether slaves or free, and were all given to
drink one Spirit.

Eph. For the perfecting of the saints unto the work of the
4:12 ministry, unto the building up of the Body of Christ.

Paul said in Ephesians 2:10 that we are the masterpiece of
God. The Greek word for masterpiece is *poiema,* a poem. The
Body of Christ as the new creation, as the organism of God, is the
poem of God. This masterpiece of God was created in Christ
through His death and resurrection with His divine element in
its all-inclusiveness. This is why this masterpiece is a poem. As
God's masterpiece we should walk in the things prepared by
God for the accomplishment of His eternal economy.

We need a vision…of the Body of Christ. This is what we are
working on and building up. When we see this vision, our seeing
will revolutionize us. It will change us, change our concept,
change our attitude, and change our realization of God's work.
(*The Practical Way to Live a Life according to the High Peak of
the Divine Revelation in the Holy Scriptures,* pp. 62-63)

Today's Reading

Our work must be a work that builds up such a Body of
Christ (Eph. 4:12, 16). This will change our idea. This will
change our view. If you have such a view, you cannot carry out
any piece of work that is not a part of the Body of Christ.

We build up the Body of Christ by growing in life (Eph. 4:15).
How much a co-worker can build up the church depends upon
how much he grows in Christ.…Our building-up work should be
the increase of the measure of Christ in us. We must grow up
into Christ, the Head, in all things.…We need to grow up into
Christ in everything, small or great.

This growing is the living of a life conformed to the death of

Christ by the power of His resurrection and by the bountiful supply of the Spirit of Jesus Christ (Phil. 3:10; 1:19b)....Such a growing affords a corporate building to the Body of Christ (Eph. 4:16).

Then all the members of the Body of Christ are joined together through every joint of the rich supply. The joints are the gifted members...(v. 11). Without their joining the members together, there can be no building....In the Body of Christ we are joined together through every joint of the rich supply.

The Body is also knit together through the operation in the measure of each one part....This includes every member of the Body of Christ. *Each one part* refers to each member of the Body. Through the growth in life and the development of gifts, each member of the Body of Christ has its own measure, which operates for the growth of the Body.

I would like to say an intimate word in fellowship, especially to the co-workers and elders among us. Do not forget that whatever you do in your locality or universally for other countries should be done in a full realization that you are building up the Body of Christ. You may have a real burden to take care of the church in your locality, yet you should always realize that you are not doing a work just for the building up of the work. When you are working to take care of the church, always keep a view of the Body. You should say, "Lord, what I am doing here is not for this, but for Your Body. I am under Your sovereign assignment, or arrangement, to work in this locality. It seems that I am doing a work to build up the local church here. But, Lord, actually I am not doing things to just build up the local church here in my locality. What I am doing, Lord, is altogether for the building up of Your Body." (*The Practical Way to Live a Life according to the High Peak of the Divine Revelation in the Holy Scriptures,* pp. 63-64, 57-58)

Further Reading: The Practical Way to Live a Life according to the High Peak of the Divine Revelation in the Holy Scriptures, ch. 6; The Divine and Mystical Realm, ch. 6

Enlightenment and inspiration: _____

_____

_____

_____

Morning Nourishment

Eph. One Body and one Spirit, even as also you were called
4:4 in one hope of your calling.

1 Cor. The cup of blessing which we bless, is it not the fellow-
10:16-17 ship of the blood of Christ? The bread which we break, is it not the fellowship of the body of Christ? Seeing that there is one bread, we who are many are one Body; for we all partake of the one bread.

Col. And when this letter is read among you, cause that it
4:16 be read in the church of the Laodiceans also, and that you also read the one from Laodicea.

According to Ephesians chapter four, the issue of the union of the Spirit of God and the spirit of the believers is the building up of the Body of Christ. This building is not of human work, nor is it a forming together of a group of people by man's natural way. Hence, it has nothing to do with man's work, effort, ways, ideas, moral teachings, philosophy, or any religious system or activities. God's eternal economy is to obtain the Body of Christ. Any work outside of this is not on the central lane of God's eternal economy. (*The Issue of the Union of the Consummated Spirit of the Triune God and the Regenerated Spirit of the Believers*, p. 49)

Today's Reading

Most of the work in today's Christianity is human work, is natural, and has nothing to do with the building up of the Body of Christ. Some people may say that Christianity also preaches the gospel and saves sinners. However, preaching the gospel and saving sinners...involve many important matters....Paul preached the gospel by supplying the person being saved by him with the Spirit of God, so that within him he might have God, the life of God, and also Christ. After that, Paul immediately told the person that his first life had already been crucified with Christ; now he needed to be buried, which is to be baptized. Not only so, Paul also told him that he was already resurrected with Christ, and his every move and action needed to have the newness of life (Rom. 6:4)....[But] today in their preaching of the gospel, people preach mainly that man must have something to rely on, that man must have religion....They also preach that Christians living on the earth have consolation and hope, and that after they die they will go to heaven. The religionists like to go to heaven, but our God likes to tabernacle among men on the earth (John 1:14; Rev. 21:3). At the end of the Bible we are told that the New Jerusalem will descend from heaven to the earth (Rev. 21:2)....What Christianity preaches today is according to man's thought, morality, and philosophy and differs greatly from what Paul preached. The gospel that Paul preached was according to the revelation of God for the building up of the Body of Christ. We are not merely preaching the gospel and saving sinners; we are saving sinners to become members of Christ, living members of the Body of Christ. (*The Issue of the Union of the Consummated Spirit of the Triune God and the Regenerated Spirit of the Believers,* pp. 49-50)

In speaking of the universal building, we must be careful to distinguish such building from organization. Although we are absolutely for the proper building, we are opposed to organization. The churches will be built together universally, but this does not mean that they will be universally organized.

According to the truth of the Body, the Body is universally one....Because each local church is part of the Body universally, no local church should be isolated from the others. This is especially true today with modern means of communication and transportation that permit the rapid spread of news and information around the world....The Body is receiving a continual transfusion. If we isolate ourselves from the other churches, we cut ourselves off both from the transfusion and from the circulation of life in the Body. Such a thing violates the law of the Body. Although we must shun organization, we need to be built up universally as the one Body. (*Life-study of Ephesians,* p. 739)

Further Reading: The Issue of the Union of the Consummated Spirit of the Triune God and the Regenerated Spirit of the Believers, ch. 4; *The Practical Points concerning Blending,* ch. 4

Enlightenment and inspiration: _____

_____
_____
_____

Morning Nourishment

Rev.   ...What you see write in a scroll and send *it* to the
1:11-12   seven churches: to Ephesus and to Smyrna....And I
          turned to see the voice that spoke with me; and
          when I turned, I saw seven golden lampstands.
21:2   And I saw the holy city, New Jerusalem, coming
          down out of heaven from God, prepared as a bride
          adorned for her husband.

The universal Body of Christ is the house of God, that is, the
kingdom of God, appearing in various cities as local churches. The
Bible shows us that one city should have only one church for the
sake of keeping the oneness and preventing division (Acts 8:1; 13:1;
Rev. 1:4, 11). Deuteronomy 12:5-18 clearly tells us that when the Israelites arrived in the good land, they could not choose a place of
worship as they liked. They needed to go to the place where God
had placed His name, which was the place where God would build
His dwelling place. The Israelites needed to worship God there.

Today the practice of the church that God desires is the same as
this in principle, that is, one city having only one church for the
keeping of the oneness. One cannot say that he is not satisfied with
the church in a certain locality and then start another meeting on
the next street with a few of his more intimate brothers. Because
Christianity is not willing to be restricted by one city having only
one church, today's situation has become confused and divided.
(*The Issue of the Union of the Consummated Spirit of the Triune
God and the Regenerated Spirit of the Believers,* pp. 84-85)

Today's Reading

The local churches in the various localities are scattered in different places by geography, yet they are not divided by any doctrine or
matter (1 Cor. 1:10-13). Some people suggest that the local churches
should be autonomous and that the churches should be inde-
pendent. However,...to be autonomous is the biggest division.

In the practice of the church, although there are many local
churches, they all take God's eternal economy as their center to
bear the unique testimony of Christ. They do not teach any

doctrine that is unrelated to God's economy and has nothing to do with the testimony of Christ. In 1 Timothy chapter one Paul wanted Timothy to remain in Ephesus to charge certain ones not to teach things that are different from God's economy (vv. 3-4). In the practice of the church, we should not teach any doctrine that is unrelated to God's economy and has nothing to do with the testimony of Christ. If we do, this will cause division. (*The Issue of the Union of the Consummated Spirit of the Triune God and the Regenerated Spirit of the Believers,* pp. 85, 87)

God desires to build all [the] regenerated children of God together as one in Christ. Thus, these dear ones should not be individual, separated, and scattered, but should be gathered together in their localities to be the local churches (Rev. 1:11).

We may think that the local churches are the goal of God's economy. However, they are not the goal, but the procedure God takes to reach the goal of His economy.…Since the time of Brother Nee the local churches have become a very precious item in our Christian life. Some of the saints may be disappointed when they hear that the local churches are not God's goal. Nevertheless, if we are just in the local churches and do not go on, we are far off from God's goal.…According to Ephesians 1:22-23, the goal of God's economy is the church, which is Christ's Body.

Eventually, the book of Revelation does have a consummation.…In the first chapter we see the seven lampstands. But in the last two chapters we see only one city. Eventually, the local churches will be over. Only the Body will remain and remain forever, and this Body of Christ is the unique tabernacle as God's dwelling place on this earth, the unique Bride of the Lamb (Rev. 21:2-3).…Therefore, we must pay much more attention to the Body of Christ than to the local churches. (*The Practical Points concerning Blending,* pp. 9-10, 23-24)

Further Reading: The Issue of the Union of the Consummated Spirit of the Triune God and the Regenerated Spirit of the Believers, ch. 6; The Practical Points concerning Blending, chs. 1, 3

Enlightenment and inspiration: _____

_____

_____

_____

Hymns, #831

1 The unity of Church is but
  The saints in oneness living;
  The Spirit which indwelleth them
  This oneness ever giving.
  Thus it is realized and called
  The unity of Spirit;
  'Tis based upon the common faith
  Which all the saints inherit.

2 This precious faith of all the saints,
  Is constituted solely
  Of Christ and His redemptive work,
  Which are unique and holy.
  In this the saints are truly one,
  Together all agreeing,
  And it is from this common faith
  The Church came into being.

3 The Church within the universe
  Is one as Christ's possession;
  The Church must therefore locally
  Be one in her expression;
  For all her elements are one—
  One God, one Lord, one Spirit,
  One faith, baptism, Body too,
  One hope all saints inherit.

4 This oneness is the Church's ground,
  The ground of common standing,
  The only ground of unity
  The Spirit is demanding.
  The Church in actual practice thus
  May keep her vital union,
  And her expressions locally
  Be built up in communion.

5 Lord, help us ever strive to keep
  This unity by taking
  The Church's ground of unity,
  The Body-life partaking,
  That all Thy heart's profound desire
  May fully be effected,
  And God's eternal purpose may
  Completely be perfected.

Composition for prophecy with main point and sub-points: _____

_____

_____

_____

_____

_____

_____

_____

_____

_____

_____

_____

_____

_____

_____

_____

_____

_____

_____

_____

_____

_____

_____

_____

_____

_____

_____

_____

_____

_____

_____

_____

_____

_____

_____

_____

Discerning the Destroyers of the Divine Building to Remain in the Lord's Recovery of the Divine Building

Scripture Reading: 1 Cor. 3:12-17

Day 1, **I. We need to see God's intention, Satan's strat-**
Day 2, **egy, and the Lord's recovery:**
Day 3,   A. God's intention in His economy is to dispense
&   Christ with all His riches into His believers
Day 4   chosen by God for the constitution and building
               up of the Body of Christ, the church, to consum-
               mate the New Jerusalem as God's ultimate
               building for the full expression of the processed
               Triune God (Eph. 3:8-10).
             B. Satan's strategy to destroy the divine building is
               versus the Lord's recovery of the divine building:
               1. Satan's strategy is to produce many substi-
                  tutes for Christ; the Lord's recovery is the
                  recovery of Christ as our center, reality, life,
                  and everything (1 Cor. 1:22-23; Col. 1:18b;
                  Rev. 2:4, 7, 17; 3:20).
               2. Satan's strategy is to divide the Body of Christ;
                  the Lord's recovery is the recovery of the
                  oneness of the Body of Christ (1 Cor. 1:10-13;
                  John 17:11b, 21; Eph. 4:3-4a; Rev. 1:11).
               3. Satan's strategy is to kill the function of all
                  the members of Christ's Body by the clergy-
                  laity system; the Lord's recovery is the
                  recovery of the function of all the members
                  of the Body of Christ (2:6; Eph. 4:15-16;
                  1 Cor. 14:4b, 26, 31).

II. We must discern the destroyers of the divine building, the workers of lawlessness, who are usurped by Satan in his strategy against the Lord's recovery of Christ as everything for the building up of His Body through the functioning of all His members (Phil. 1:9; 2 Cor. 11:14-15; Matt. 7:23):

A. To destroy God's building is to ruin, corrupt, defile, and mar the temple of God; it is to build with the worthless materials of wood (the natural man), grass (the flesh), and stubble (lifelessness) (1 Cor. 3:17, 12b).

B. Using any doctrine that differs from the fundamental teachings of the apostles (Acts 2:42) or any ways and efforts that contradict God's nature, Christ's redemptive work, and the Spirit's transforming work is to corrupt, ruin, defile, and mar the temple of God, that is, to destroy it.

C. When the Lord Jesus comes back, our building work will be tested by His holy fire; if our work is done in Christ, with Christ, for Christ, and is even Christ Himself, it will pass the test of fire (1 Cor. 3:12-15).

Day 5
&
Day 6

III. **The destroyers of the divine building are those who blow the wind of divisive teachings by stressing things other than the central teaching concerning God's economy (Eph. 4:14; 1 Tim. 1:3-4):**

A. Teaching different things rather than the unique ministry of God's economy tears down God's building and annuls God's economy (vv. 3-4).

B. There is only one ministry that ever builds up and never destroys—this is God's economy; the only way that we can be preserved in the eternal oneness is to teach the same thing in God's economy (Eph. 4:11-12; 2 Cor. 4:1).

IV. **The destroyers of the divine building are those who preach and teach heresies (2 Pet. 2:1; 2 John 7-11):**

A. Those who teach heresies concerning the person of Christ are antichrists, denying both the person of the Lord as the Master and His redemption, by which the Lord purchased the believers;

to deny that the man Jesus is God is a great heresy (v. 7; 1 John 2:18, 22-23; 4:2-3).

B. The apostle warned the believers to watch for themselves lest they be influenced by the heresies and lose the things of the truth; we must reject those who deny the conception and deity of Christ, not receiving them into our house nor greeting them (2 John 8-11).

C. If we would not be led astray by the heresies but would abide faithfully in the truth concerning the wonderful and all-inclusive Christ, who is both God and man, both our Creator and our Redeemer, we will enjoy in Him the Triune God to the fullest extent as our full reward, even today on earth (v. 8).

V. The destroyers of the divine building are those who are factious, sectarian (Titus 3:10):

A. A factious man is a heretical, sectarian man who causes divisions by forming parties in the church according to his own opinions; in order to maintain good order in the church, a factious, divisive person should be refused, rejected, after a first and second admonition.

B. Because such divisiveness is contagious, this rejection is for the church's profit that contact with the divisive one may be stopped (cf. Num. 6:6-7).

VI. The destroyers of the divine building are those who make divisions (Rom. 16:17):

A. In Romans 14 Paul was liberal and gracious regarding the receiving of those who differ in doctrine or practice; however, in Romans 16:17 he was unyielding and resolute in saying that we must "mark those who make divisions and causes of stumbling contrary to the teaching which you have learned, and turn away from them."

B. The Lord hates "one who injects discord among brothers" (Prov. 6:16, 19).

VII. The destroyers of the divine building are those who are ambitious for position (3 John 9):

A. The self-exalting and domineering Diotrophes is an evil pattern of someone who is ambitious for position and "loves to be first" among the saints (v. 9).

B. We should never hunt to be the first in any work for the Lord; this is the insidious work of hidden ambition to compete with others to be the first.

VIII. The destroyers of the divine building are those who are wolves, not sparing the flock, and those who speak perverted things to draw away the believers after them (Acts 20:29-30):

A. The intrinsic need in the Lord's recovery is for a remnant of His people to build up the church as the kingdom of God, to "build up the wall," to protect the church from the destroyers of God's building (Neh. 2:4, 10, 17-20).

B. We must shepherd the flock of God by declaring to them all the counsel of God, all of God's economy; under the Lord's shepherding, all the evil persons who disturb God's people are kept away from them so that they can dwell in peace and safety to be mingled with God and bound together in oneness (Acts 20:26-35; Ezek. 33:1-11; 34:25; cf. Zech. 2:8; 11:7).

Morning Nourishment

1 Cor. ...I have laid a foundation, and another builds upon
3:10-13 it. But <u>let each man take heed how he builds upon</u> it.
For another foundation no one is able to lay besides
that which is laid, which is Jesus Christ. But if anyone builds upon the foundation gold, silver, precious
stones, wood, grass, stubble, the work of each will
become manifest,...of what sort it is.
17 If anyone destroys the temple of God, God will destroy
him; for the temple of God is holy, *and* such are you.

In 1 Corinthians 3:10 Paul says, "But let each man take heed
how he builds upon it." The church must be built with gold, silver,
and precious stones. However, there is much possibility that we
may build with wood, grass, and stubble. Hence, each of us must
take heed how he builds, that is, with what materials he builds.

We must take heed not to build with anything other than
Christ. This means that whenever we give a message or a testimony, or whenever we have fellowship with others, we must be
careful not to give others anything except Christ. Furthermore,
the Christ we share should not be a doctrinal Christ, but a Christ
whom we have experienced. We should minister not merely the
knowledge of Christ or the doctrine of Christ, but Christ Himself.
In everything we do in the church life, we must take heed not to
minister anything other than the Christ we have experienced.

Paul seems to be telling the Corinthians, "Brothers, be careful
<u>how you build on Christ as the foundation.</u> God desires a building,
a temple. Take heed that you do not build with your Greek culture, philosophy, and wisdom. Likewise, those with a background
in Judaism must be careful not to build with Jewish culture, religion, and concepts. Instead, we all must learn to minister Christ
to others." This is what it means to take heed how we build on the
foundation already laid. (*Life-study of 1 Corinthians,* p. 232)

Today's Reading

It is very easy to build on the foundation with something natural or something of our culture, even though we have no intention

to do so and are not aware of what we are doing. For example, we may build with something American, Chinese, or German. Furthermore, we may also build with certain elements common to the culture of our particular region. If we minister to others in this way, we are very careless. We are not taking heed how we build....It is crucial for us all to learn to build upon Christ as the foundation with the Christ we have experienced in a practical way. There is a lack of such building among us. I am concerned that many brothers and sisters will simply repeat messages in a doctrinal way. What is urgently needed is the actual, practical, present, and living Christ in our experience. To build with such a Christ is to take heed how we build.

[Here Paul is saying], "Brothers, instead of building the church in your locality, you are destroying it and tearing it down. You are not building with gold, silver, and precious stones, but with wood, grass, and stubble. You are building with your Greek natural man and your Greek culture, philosophy, wisdom, habits, and customs. Thus, you are destroying the temple of God and will suffer God's destruction....Take heed to avoid building with your Greek humanity and culture. You need to avoid everything Greek and be in the mingled spirit to minister the golden nature of God the Father into others and also to minister the silver of the cross of Christ. The result will be precious stones, a metabolic change produced by the transforming work of the Holy Spirit." This is to build with the Triune God upon Christ as the unique foundation.

It is significant that Paul mentions only three categories of precious materials—gold, silver, and precious stones—for these correspond to the three of the Triune God....This is the experience of the Triune God becoming the supply for us to minister to the saints and the materials for the building up of the church. (*Life-study of 1 Corinthians,* pp. 232-233, 237)

Further Reading: Life-study of 1 Corinthians, msg. 26; *The Basic Principles for the Practice of the God-ordained Way; Satan's Strategy Against the Church*

Enlightenment and inspiration: _____

_____

_____

_____

Morning Nourishment

1 Cor. **For another foundation no one is able to lay besides**
3:11-12 **that which is laid, which is Jesus Christ. But if any-**
one builds upon the foundation gold, silver, precious
stones, wood, grass, stubble.

Wood, grass, and stubble signify the knowledge, realization, and attainments which come from the believers' background (such as Judaism or other religions, philosophy, or culture) and the natural way of living (which is mostly in the soul and is the natural life). Wood may be in contrast to gold, signifying the nature of the natural man; grass may be in contrast to silver, signifying the fallen man, the man of the flesh (1 Pet. 1:24), unredeemed by Christ; and stubble may be in contrast to precious stones, signifying the work and living which issue from an earthen source, without any transformation by the Holy Spirit. All these worthless materials are the product of the believers' natural man together with what they have collected from their background. In God's economy these materials are fit only to be burned (1 Cor. 3:13). (*Life-study of 1 Corinthians*, p. 241)

Today's Reading

Specifically and practically, wood here refers to the human nature of the Greeks. By nature the Greeks are very philosophical. I believe they even philosophized concerning Christ. Thus, wood refers to their nature, their natural makeup. In the same principle, wood denotes what we are according to our natural makeup....We should not build [the church] with our nature, with our natural makeup.

Grass signifies the unredeemed man of the flesh....To build the church with grass is to build it with what we are in our natural being. For example, the leader of the Brethren assembly I attended in Chefoo was a very slow and steady person. He always walked slowly, carefully, and deliberately. Once in teaching the Bible he said that God always does things slowly. Because of the influence of this leader, almost everyone in that assembly learned to be slow.... In the area of the meeting hall, they walked very slowly....Prayers in the meetings were offered in a very slow way. That entire

Brethren assembly was according to the natural being of the leader. This is an illustration of what it means to build the church with grass.

To build with grass is to build with what we are and with what we prefer. Suppose a particular person has a strong preference for speaking in tongues. To seek to promote tongues-speaking is to build with grass. Whenever we build according to what we are in our natural being or according to our natural preference, we build with grass.

Stubble signifies the work and living which issue from an earthen source. Stubble is altogether without life. To build with stubble is even worse than building with wood and grass. Jealousy, strife, envy, gossip, and criticism are all aspects of stubble.

It is very difficult among Christians today to find the proper building materials. Where can you find gold, silver, and precious stones? However, there is an abundance of wood, grass, and stubble....In almost any Christian group you can find wood, grass, stubble; that is, you can find the building according to the natural makeup, the natural being, and the characteristics of earthly living. In particular, in 1 Corinthians 3 wood, grass, and stubble refer to the Greek nature, the Greek being, and the evil of the Greek way of living, especially as these things were expressed among the believers in Corinth.

In chapter three Paul charges the saints not to lay anything or anyone other than Christ as the unique foundation. This means that we must not exalt anyone or anything in place of Christ. If we exalt someone or something instead of Christ, we lay another foundation. Paul also charges us to take heed how we build upon Christ as the unique foundation. The Corinthians were not to build with their Greek nature, their Greek self, or their Greek jealousy, strife, and criticism. In other words, they were not to build the church with anything Greek. (*Life-study of 1 Corinthians,* pp. 241-243)

Further Reading: Life-study of 1 Corinthians, msg. 27; *The Practical Points concerning Blending,* ch. 5

Enlightenment and inspiration: _____

_____

_____

_____

Morning Nourishment

1 Cor. Do you not know that you are the temple of God,
3:16-17 and *that* the Spirit of God dwells in you? If anyone
destroys the temple of God, God will destroy him;
for the temple of God is holy, *and* such are you.

As we become gold, silver, and precious stones, we are built
up. Building is a matter of growth and transformation. The more
we grow, the more we are rescued from our natural being. Then
wherever we may be, we can easily be one with the saints. This is
building. If we have been built up in a genuine way, there will be
no opinions, disputations, strifes, comparisons, preferences, or
choices. We shall simply be for the Lord's Body and desire to be
part of the Body. No matter where we may go, we shall be one
with every saint. This is what it means to be built with gold, silver, and precious stones.

The majority of today's Christians are divided. It is difficult
even to find two who have been built together in a proper way.
The reason for the division and the lack of building is that the
believers remain in their natural life, in their natural being, and
in their worldly aspirations. Many still have their own preferences, desires, and choices. As a result, it is impossible for them
to be truly one. Therefore there cannot be the practical Body life
among them. (*Life-study of 1 Corinthians*, pp. 282-283)

Today's Reading

In 1 Corinthians 3:16 and 17...Paul warns us not to destroy
God's temple....The temple in verse 16 refers to the believers
collectively in a certain locality, as in Corinth. The unique spiritual temple of God in the universe has its expression in many localities on earth. Each expression is a temple of God in that
locality....The temple is built up with the believers in a practical
way. Regarding the building, first we must gather the materials,
and then the materials become part of the building.

In chapter three Paul warns the Corinthians to take heed
how they build. On the positive side, he indicates that they
should build on the foundation with gold, silver, and precious

stones. On the negative side, he warns them about destroying the temple of God. The Greek word rendered destroy also means ruin, corrupt, defile, mar. To build with wood, grass, and stubble is to ruin, to mar, God's building. According to the context of chapter three, we may destroy the temple either by laying a foundation other than Christ, or by building on the foundation with wood, grass, and stubble. For the Corinthians to say that they were of Paul, Apollos, or Cephas was to lay another foundation and thus to mar the temple. Furthermore, to build with natural things was also to ruin the temple of God.

If we consider the last verses of chapter three according to the context of the first three chapters of this Epistle, we shall see that Paul's concept is that saying we are of someone is to destroy the church. Paul seems to be saying here, "The church is in the process of being built up. Some parts have already been built. Do not destroy the church. Do not mar it, ruin it, or defile it. If you build the church with your natural being or your natural makeup, you defile the church. You also ruin the church when you say that you are of Apollos, Cephas, or Paul. If you destroy the church in this way, God will destroy you." On the one hand, to be destroyed by God is to be deprived of the blessing. It is to lack the feeding, the drinking, the eating, the planting, the watering, and the growing. It is also to miss the opportunity to gain the gold, silver, and precious stones. On the other hand, to be destroyed is to be judged by fire and to have our work consumed. However, if we build with gold, silver, and precious stones, our work will remain, and we shall receive a reward (v. 14).

I encourage you to pray-read these verses in the light of what we have covered in this message. If you do this, you will be nourished and have the divine element infused into you. Then you will experience more transformation, and the church will have more building. (*Life-study of 1 Corinthians,* pp. 284-286)

Further Reading: Life-study of 1 Corinthians, msg. 32; *How to Be a Co-worker and an Elder and How to Fulfill Their Obligations,* ch. 6

Enlightenment and inspiration: _____

_____

_____

Morning Nourishment

1 Cor. The work of each will become manifest; for the day
3:13-15 will declare *it*, because it is revealed by fire, and
the fire itself will prove each one's work, of what
sort it is. If anyone's work which he has built upon
the foundation remains, he will receive a reward; if
anyone's work is consumed, he will suffer loss, but
he himself will be saved, yet so as through fire.
Matt. And then I will declare to them: I never knew you.
7:23 Depart from Me, you workers of lawlessness.

In 1 Corinthians 3:13..."the day"...refers to the day of Christ's
second coming, when He will judge all His believers (4:5; Matt.
25:19-30; 2 Cor. 5:10; Rev. 22:12).

The fire in verse 13 denotes the fire of the Lord's judgment
(Mal. 3:2; 4:1; 2 Thes. 1:8; Heb. 6:8), which will cause each believer's
work to be manifest and will try and test his work....All the work
of wood, grass, and stubble will not be able to stand that test and
will be burned.

In verse 14...the work that remains must be that of gold, silver,
and precious stones, the product of faithful ministers of Christ.
Such a work will be rewarded by the coming and judging Lord.
Reward is based upon the believer's work after being saved. It differs from salvation, which is based upon faith in the Lord and His
redemptive work. (*Life-study of 1 Corinthians,* pp. 237-238)

Today's Reading

Realizing the seriousness of using natural things to build up
the church, I have earnestly endeavored, by the Lord's mercy, not to
bring Chinese things into the Lord's recovery in this country. Moreover, I certainly do not want anything of what I am to influence the
building of the church. None of us should build the church according to what we are in our natural being. We should not allow anything of our natural being to be put into the church....If the church
expresses the natural makeup or natural being of the leading ones,
this indicates that, at least to some extent, the church has been
built with grass. Something of the unredeemed natural man has

been put into the church. This is an element which has not been redeemed, terminated, and replaced by Christ.

In chapter three Paul was actually telling the Corinthian believers, "You are plants on God's farm. Now you need to grow Christ. The more you grow, the more you will become gold, silver, and precious stones for God's building. Do not lay any foundation other than Christ. Do not exalt anything, anyone, or any doctrine or practice. Simply build upon the all-inclusive Christ as the unique foundation already laid. But take heed not to build upon this Christ with anything Greek; rather build with the Father's nature and the Son's redemption which will result in the Spirit's transformation. Then the church will be golden and full of silver and precious stones."

In verse 15 Paul issues a word of warning....The work of wood, grass, and stubble is fit only to be burned. This is the work which shall be consumed by the Lord's judging fire at His return.

When Paul says, "He will suffer loss," he means loss of reward, not loss of salvation. To suffer loss here absolutely does not mean to perish. The salvation which we have received in Christ is not by our works (Titus 3:5) and is eternal, unchangeable in nature (Heb. 5:9; John 10:28-29). Hence, those believers whose Christian works will not be approved by the judging Lord and who will suffer the loss of reward will still be saved. God's salvation to all believers as a free gift is for eternity, whereas the Lord's reward to those whose Christian works are approved by Him is for the kingdom age. The reward is an incentive for their Christian work, and it is not given to all believers.

Although those believers whose Christian works will not be approved by the Lord at His coming back will be saved, they will be saved so as through fire. Through fire surely indicates punishment. ...This word should be a solemn warning to us today concerning our Christian works. (*Life-study of 1 Corinthians*, pp. 244-246)

Further Reading: Life-study of 1 Corinthians, msg. 27; *How to Be a Co-worker and an Elder and How to Fulfill Their Obligations*, ch. 6

Enlightenment and inspiration: _____

_____

_____

_____

Morning Nourishment

1 Tim. **Even as I exhorted you...to remain in Ephesus in**
1:3-4 **order that you might charge certain ones not to teach
different things nor to give heed to myths and unending genealogies, which produce questionings rather
than God's economy, which is in faith.**

Throughout...church history, the divisions, confusions, and
problems...were all due to a ministry. Whatever you minister produces something. If you minister the heavens, something heavenly
will be produced. If you minister earthly things, surely the issue,
the coming out, will be earthly. The many divisions and confusions
among the Christians today all come from one source—a ministry.
The Presbyterian denomination or division came out of the ministry of the presbytery. The Baptist division came out of the ministry
of baptism by immersion. All the different kinds of Christian
groups come out of different ministries. A ministry is mainly a
teaching. We must realize that the teaching which a Christian
teaches ministers something....Ministry in the biblical usage
means to serve people with something....We may say that a certain minister who speaks for an hour ministers nothing to people.
This means that according to Christ he ministered nothing, but according to the facts, that minister did minister something. He ministered something wrong, something bad, or something low to
people. I hope we can see that ministry produces problems, ministry produces division, and ministry produces confusion. (*Elders'
Training, Book 3: The Way to Carry Out the Vision*, pp. 41-42)

Today's Reading

[The problem of different ministries] is why Paul wrote 1 Timothy in the midst of a confusing environment and after many years
of his work with his co-workers. This Epistle is altogether an inocu-
lation. Poison after poison was injected into the Christian church
while the church was going on. At the conclusion of his writing
ministry, Paul wrote 1 Timothy to inoculate the church against all
these poisons. In the opening word of this Epistle,...[the] phrase
"not to teach different things" [1:3] seems so simple....We may not

think that this is serious, but actually it is more than serious. It kills people to teach different things. To teach different things tears down God's building and annuls God's entire economy. We all must realize that even a small amount of teaching different things destroys the recovery….We must realize that ministry is "terrible." Your speaking can build up or destroy.

[Paul left Timothy] in Ephesus to charge certain ones not to teach different things. What then…is the unique thing which all the Christian teachers should teach? Christian teachers today teach many things such as the presbytery, baptism by immersion, the episcopalian way, holiness, how to preach the gospel, and the way to teach the Bible. We would all agree that to teach the way of Judaism is surely wrong, but what about teaching how to preach the gospel? What is wrong with preaching the gospel? We must realize that even the teaching to preach the gospel creates division. This is wrong. There is only one ministry which always builds up, edifies, and perfects with no destruction at all. There is only one unique ministry that is justified, promoted, uplifted, and even glorified in the New Testament. In 1 Timothy 1:4 Paul went on to tell Timothy what those ones who were teaching different things should be occupied with—God's economy….There is only one ministry that ever builds up and that never destroys—this is God's economy.

The only way that can preserve us in the recovery is the unique ministry….The ministry of the new covenant is only to minister the Triune God, processed, to be dispensed into His chosen people as life and life supply to produce members of Christ to form the Body to express the Triune God. This is the New Testament economy. To teach anything, even good things and scriptural things, which is even a little bit apart from God's New Testament economy will still issue in division, and that will be very much used by the subtle one, the evil one. We must, therefore, be on the alert. (*Elders' Training, Book 3: The Way to Carry Out the Vision,* pp. 42-44, 48-49)

Further Reading: Elders' Training, Book 3: The Way to Carry Out the Vision, ch. 4

__Enlightenment and inspiration:__ _____
_____
_____
_____

Morning Nourishment

Rom.   Now I exhort you, brothers, to mark those who make
16:17   divisions and causes of stumbling contrary to the teach-
      ing which you have learned, and turn away from them.
Gal.   And *this*, because of the false brothers, brought in secret-
2:4   ly, who stole in to spy out our freedom which we have in
      Christ Jesus, that they might bring us into slavery.

We need to be very clear that the foundation of all the denominations and the factor that produces each denomination are their
different ministries. If all the Christians today would be willing
for the Lord to take away their different ministries, they would all
be one. The basic factor of all the divisions, their very root, is different ministries....This thing crept in as early as the time of Paul
[Gal. 2]. Paul, Peter, and James were all there, and a ministry of
another kind was trying to come in. In 1 Timothy 1 Paul charged
Timothy to remain in Ephesus to take care of one thing: to charge
certain ones not to teach different things, which means not to
teach according to another ministry (vv. 3-4). At that time the different teaching was the teaching of the law. In Galatians 2 what
was trying to creep in was the law. (*Elders' Training, Book 1: The
Ministry of the New Testament*, pp. 14-15)

Today's Reading

In the four Gospels Jesus Christ carried out God's ministry, and
in the first part of Acts, Peter continued that ministry. Then in the
second part of Acts, Paul's ministry was a continuation of Peter's to
carry out God's New Testament ministry. Nevertheless, when the
Judaizing believers were strong in teaching the law, Peter became
weak. Peter was afraid of those who came down from James (Gal.
2:11-12). This also indicates that James was a strong figure, a
strong character, in tolerating the teaching of the law in the New
Testament age.

In Antioch Paul was facing the number one apostle, Peter, and
he was facing representatives of the most influential apostle,
James....Undoubtedly, it was hard for him. Nevertheless, for the
sake of the truth, Paul did not tolerate that situation....He closed

the door to the different ministries that were creeping in, and God honored what Paul did in that situation.

According to the New Testament and according to church history, from that time onward Peter did not play an important role in God's New Testament economy....After not too long a time, in A.D. 70, God destroyed Jerusalem (Matt. 24:1-2), which was the base of Peter's work and the base of James' influence. He tore down the whole thing, leaving no stone upon another, destroying it. Not only was that a judgment on the rebellious Israel, but it was also the destruction of the base of Peter's work and of James' influence.... However, Paul's ministry and his influence remained. God did not allow different ministries and other influences.

We need to see this principle throughout the entire Christian era. All the troubles, divisions, and confusions came from the one source of the tolerance of different ministries. Many Christian teachers have known the peril of different ministries; nevertheless, they have tolerated them. There has been a tolerance of different ministries. In the Lord's recovery, for the long run, we should not believe that this kind of creeping in of the different ministries would never take place. Rather, we must be on the alert. Such a peril is ahead of us. If we are not watchful, if we are careless, in one way or another the enemy would creepingly use some means, some ways, to bring in different ministries. Such a thing would end the Lord's recovery.

If you look at today's situation, you will realize that there are many different ministries in addition to this unique New Testament ministry. If you could take away all the different ministries and leave only the unique ministry of the New Testament, all the denominations, all the different groups, and all the divisions, would disappear. There would be no division and no confusion. (*Elders' Training, Book 1: The Ministry of the New Testament*, pp. 15-17, 70-71)

Further Reading: Elders' Training, Book 1: The Ministry of the New Testament, ch. 1; *Life-study of Ezekiel,* msg. 16; *How to Be a Co-worker and an Elder and How to Fulfill Their Obligations,* ch. 4

Enlightenment and inspiration: _____

_____

_____

_____

Hymns, #839

1 Lord, Thou art a potter skilled
And a glorious builder too,
Molding for Thy vessel great,
Building with Thy house in view.
I am both a man of clay
And a new-made living stone,
That Thy vessel I may be
And the temple Thou wouldst own.

2 Though of clay Thou madest us,
Thou wouldst have us be transformed;
With Thy life as purest gold,
Unto precious stones conformed.
We shall, through Thy building work,
Then become Thy loving Bride,
In one Body joined to Thee,
That Thy heart be satisfied.

3 What Thy heart desires and loves
Are not precious stones alone,
But together these to build
For Thy glory, for Thy home.
Thou, the all-inclusive Christ,
Dost a builded Church require,
That Thy glorious riches may
Radiate their light entire.

4 Not the person spiritual
In an individual way,
But the corporate life expressed
Will Thy heart's desire display.
Members separate and detached
Ne'er express Thee perfectly,
But Thy Body tempered, built,
Ever shall Thy fulness be.

5 Build me, Lord, with other saints,
Independence ne'er allow,
But according to Thy plan
Fitly frame and join me now.
In experience not my boast,
Nor in gifts would be my pride;
For Thy building I give all,
That Thou may be glorified.

Composition for prophecy with main point and sub-points: _____

_____

_____

_____

_____

_____

_____

_____

_____

_____

_____

_____

_____

_____

_____

_____

_____

_____

_____

_____

_____

_____

_____

_____

_____

_____

_____

_____

_____

_____

_____

_____

_____

_____

_____

The New Jerusalem—
the Ultimate Consummation
of the Building of God

Scripture Reading: John 1:14; 2:19-21; Rev. 21:3, 22; 2 Sam. 7:12-14a; Rom. 1:3-4; 8:28-29

Day 1 & Day 2

I. The New Jerusalem is the ultimate consummation of the building of God into man and of man into God, the building of a great corporate God-man as the mutual abode of God and man, the universal incorporation of the processed and consummated Triune God with the processed and consummated tripartite man (John 1:14; 2:19-21; Rev. 21:3, 22).

II. Second Samuel 7:12-14a is a prophecy in typology revealing that the desire of God's heart is the building of God into man (God becoming man) and the building of man into God (man becoming God) for the building of a great corporate God-man, the New Jerusalem:

A. The seed of David (v. 12) becoming the Son of God (v. 14a) is the building of God into man and the building of man into God for the building of God's house, the mutual abode of God and man (v. 13); this is the fulfillment of the greatest prophecy in the Bible (Rom. 1:3-4; Matt. 16:18).

B. Christ "came out of the seed of David according to the flesh" (building God into man in incarnation), and He "was designated the Son of God" (building man into God in resurrection) (Rom. 1:3-4):

1. By His incarnation Christ, the only begotten Son of God in His divinity (John 1:18), built God into man, into David's lineage, to become the seed of David, the son of David.

2. In resurrection Christ's humanity was deified, sonized, meaning that He became the Son of God not only in His divinity but also in His

humanity; in resurrection He was designated the Son of God, made the firstborn
Son of God, possessing both divinity and
humanity (Rom. 1:3-4; 8:29).

3. If a seed dies by being buried in the soil, it
will eventually sprout, grow, and blossom in
resurrection, because the operation of the
seed's life is activated simultaneously with its
death; in resurrection Christ "blossomed" as
the firstborn Son of God, and He became
the life-giving Spirit to dispense, to build,
Himself as life into our being to be our inner
constitution (John 12:23-24; Acts 13:33;
1 Pet. 3:18).

Day 3
&
Day 4
III. **As seeds of humanity, we are becoming sons
of God with divinity, being "divinized" in our
humanity through the metabolic process of
transformation; this metabolic process is the
building up of the church as the Body of Christ
and the house of God by the building of God
into man and of man into God, consummating in the New Jerusalem as a great corporate God-man, the aggregate, the totality, of
all the sons of God (Heb. 2:10; Rev. 21:7; Rom.
8:28-29):**

A. The life of the Son of God has been implanted
into our spirit; now we, like the seed that is sown
into the earth, must pass through the process of
death and resurrection (v. 10; John 12:24-26):

1. Losing our soul-life through death causes the
outer man to be consumed, but it enables the
inner life to grow, to develop, and ultimately,
to blossom; this is resurrection (1 Cor. 15:31,
36; 2 Cor. 4:10-12, 16).

2. The more we grow in life for our transformation in life, the more we are designated the
sons of God to be deified for God's building
(1 Cor. 3:9):

a. In order to grow, we need to feed on the

guileless milk and the solid food of the word (1 Pet. 2:2; Heb. 5:12-14).

b. In order to grow, we need the watering of the gifted members (1 Cor. 3:6b; John 7:37-39; Prov. 11:25).

c. Through all the things in our environment and by our failures, our ugly self is torn down, and the Lord has a greater opportunity to work within us (Rom. 8:28-29).

d. One day this process will be completed, and for eternity we will be the same as Christ, God's firstborn Son, in our spirit, soul, and body (1 John 3:2; Rom. 8:19, 23; *Hymns,* #948, stanza 2).

B. In resurrection Christ in His humanity was designated the Son of God, and by means of such a resurrection we also are in the process of being designated sons of God (Rom. 8:11; cf. Hosea 6:1-3):

1. The process of our being designated, sonized, deified, is the process of resurrection with four main aspects—sanctification, transformation, conformation, and glorification (Rom. 6:22; 12:2; 8:29-30).

2. The key to the process of designation is resurrection, which is the indwelling Christ as the rising-up Spirit, the designating Spirit, the power of life in our spirit (John 11:25; Rom. 8:10-11; Acts 2:24; 1 Cor. 15:26; 5:4):

a. We urgently need to learn how to walk according to the spirit, to enjoy and experience the designating Spirit (Rom. 8:4, 14).

b. The more we touch the Spirit, the more we are sanctified, transformed, conformed, and glorified to become God in life and in nature but not in the Godhead for the building up of the Body of Christ to consummate the New Jerusalem (1 Cor. 12:3; Rom. 10:12; 8:15-16; Gal. 4:6).

Day 6   **IV. As we work for God today, we should participate in God's building—the constitution of the
divine element into the human element and
of the human element into the divine element (John 14:20; 15:4a; 1 John 4:15):**

A. We need God in Christ to build Himself into us,
making our heart, our intrinsic constitution, His
home (Eph. 3:16-19).

B. We need to practice one thing—to minister the
processed and consummated Triune God into
others so that He may build Himself into their
inner man; we need to pray that the Lord will
teach us to work in this way (2 Cor. 13:14; 1 Cor.
3:9a, 10, 12a).

C. When we build the church with the processed
and consummated Triune God, it is not actually
we who are building; rather, God is building
through us, using us as a means to dispense and
transmit Himself into others (Acts 9:15).

D. This building will consummate in the New Jerusalem for eternity, in which God's redeemed are
the tabernacle for God to dwell in and God Himself is the temple for His redeemed to dwell in
(Rev. 21:3, 22).

Morning Nourishment

2 Sam. When your days are fulfilled and you sleep with your
7:12-14 fathers, I will raise up your seed after you, which will
come forth from your body, and I will establish his
kingdom. It is he who will build a house for My
name, and I will establish the throne of his kingdom
forever. I will be his Father, and he will be My son....

Eph. That Christ may make His home in your hearts
3:17 through faith...

Second Samuel 7 is a very difficult portion of the Word to understand, and not many Christians have the proper view concerning it....[Nearly no one has seen] the intrinsic significance of this chapter, especially of God's word to David in verses 12 through 14a.... This chapter conveys a great prophecy, but this prophecy is unveiled through typology....It is a prophecy in typology.

In 2 Samuel 7, David, like many of us, had the mistaken concept that God needed him to build something for Him. When some hear this they may wonder how this concept can be wrong since we today are endeavoring to build up the church. Is building the church not a matter of building something for God?...Apparently we are the ones who are building the church, but actually God is the One who is building the church with Christ as the unique element. When we are about to do some building work by speaking for God, He may check with us, saying, "Do you intend to build My house? With what material will you build My house?" If we say that we are building up the church with Christ, God may ask us how much we have of Christ. This exposes our shortage of Christ. We need Christ not merely in name and in knowledge; we need the real Christ, Christ as the Spirit in resurrection. We all need more and more of Christ. (*Life-study of 1 & 2 Samuel*, pp. 159-160)

Today's Reading

The church is not built with the knowledge of the Bible. The church is built with Christ as the unique element....In 2 Samuel 7 David wanted to build God's house, but in this chapter God wanted David to realize that he needed God to build Christ into him. Thus, 2 Samuel 7 is the unveiling of a prophecy through typology showing us there is no need for us to build something for God. We simply are not able to do this. We cannot build something for God with ourselves or with our knowledge of the Bible and theology. We need God to build up Christ into our intrinsic constitution so that our entire being will be reconstituted with Christ. As a result, we are not only changed, but we are transformed from one kind of person into another.

The New Testament verse that best indicates that Christ is building Himself into us is Ephesians 3:17. Here Paul says that Christ is making His home in our hearts. This is building. What is of crucial importance today is the question concerning how much of Christ has been built into us. How much has Christ been built not only into your spirit but into your heart in order to make His home there?

Our spirit, the central part of our being, is surrounded by our heart, which is composed mainly of our mind, emotion, and will. Christ is in our spirit, but how much has Christ made His home in our heart? Most of our hearts are still vacant, not occupied, saturated, and soaked with Christ. Every day our hearts are filled with other things. As a result, Christ is imprisoned in our spirit.

Ephesians 3 indicates strongly that the Triune God is building Himself into us in Christ's making us His home. Paul bowed his knees to the Father and prayed that He would grant us, according to the riches of His glory, to be strengthened with power through His Spirit into the inner man (vv. 14, 16) so that Christ may make His home in our hearts. Here we have the Divine Trinity: the Father is the One to whom Paul prayed; the Spirit is the One who carries out the strengthening; and Christ the Son is the One who is making His home in our heart. By building Himself into our being, He makes our heart, our intrinsic constitution, His home. (*Life-study of 1 & 2 Samuel*, pp. 160-162)

Further Reading: Life-study of 1 & 2 Samuel, msg. 24

Enlightenment and inspiration: _____

_____

_____

_____

Morning Nourishment

1 Cor. But if anyone builds upon the foundation gold, silver,
3:12 precious stones, wood, grass, stubble.

Eph. For the perfecting of the saints unto the work of the
4:12 ministry, unto the building up of the Body of Christ.

16 ...All the Body...causes the growth of the Body unto
the building up of itself in love.

Matt. ...I will build My church...
16:18

In 1 Corinthians 3:12 Paul said that there are two categories of building material—wood, grass, and stubble, which are human and worldly, and gold, silver, and precious stones, which are precious treasures and transformed materials. If we build the church with wood, grass, and stubble—with the attainments that come from our natural background or with the natural way of living—we will destroy the church (v. 17). We should build the church with gold, silver, and precious stones, signifying respectively God, Christ, and the Spirit. To build the church with these materials is to build the church with the processed and consummated Triune God. When we build the church with the processed and consummated Triune God, it is not actually we who are building. Rather, God is building through us, using us as a means to dispense and transmit Himself into people. (*Life-study of 1 & 2 Samuel,* p. 162)

Today's Reading

In Matthew 16:18 the Lord Jesus said, "I will build My church." But how is the church to be built? The church is built with the Triune God: with the Father as the source, with the Son as the element, and with the Spirit as the essence. This is clearly indicated in Ephesians 4:4-6. According to these verses, the whole church, the Body of Christ, is a mingling of the human frame with the Triune God as the source, the element, and the essence. On the one hand, the gifted persons perfect the saints unto the work of the ministry so that the Body may build up itself in love. On the other hand, the processed and consummated Triune God as the source, the element, and the essence is building the church by building Himself into our being.

We need to have this realization as we are working for the Lord. It is not adequate simply to present to others some knowledge concerning God's economy and other divine, spiritual, and heavenly things. We need to dispense the Triune God into others. Through our prayer, fasting, repentance, and confession, the Triune God can fill us, saturate us, and mingle with us as our source, element, and essence. Then we can go with Him and work with Him. If we are filled with the Triune God, when we speak He will flow out and be ministered to others for their nourishment.

Second Samuel 7 is a prophecy predicting that the church will be built up by God Himself among His people in the New Testament. Christ is the One who actually builds God's house, God's temple. Christ is also the element in which and with which the church as God's house is built. In this chapter God seemed to be saying to David, "David, thus far you are still vacant and empty. Do not think that you should do something to build a house for Me. You need to realize that you need Me to build Myself into you as the Father, the Son, and the Spirit. Then you will have a house, and that house will also be My house."

The intrinsic significance of 2 Samuel 7 is that the Triune God is working Himself in His processed and consummated Trinity into His chosen people....[This] is a chapter on the Triune God working Himself into us to make us His home (Christ with the church) and to produce a seed (the all-inclusive Christ). Here we have a house and a seed. Christ is the house, and Christ is also the seed. Christ is the element, and Christ is also the issue. Christ is everything.

This Christ is both God's house and our house. Hence, we and God have a mutual abode. Christ abides in us, and we abide in Him. He and we, we and He, are mingled together as one entity. ...The whole universe is eagerly awaiting the expression of the Triune God mingled with the tripartite man through His building, which is by Himself, with Himself, in Himself, and for Himself. (*Life-study of 1 & 2 Samuel,* pp. 162-164)

Further Reading: Life-study of 1 & 2 Samuel, msg. 24

Enlightenment and inspiration: _____
_____
_____
_____

Morning Nourishment

2 Sam. When your days are fulfilled and you sleep with your
7:12-14 fathers, I will raise up your seed after you, which will
come forth from your body, and I will establish his
kingdom. It is he who will build a house for My name,
and I will establish the throne of his kingdom forever. I
will be his Father, and he will be My son....

Rom. Concerning His Son, who came out of the seed of David
1:3-4 according to the flesh, who was designated the Son of
God in power according to the Spirit of holiness out
of the resurrection of the dead, Jesus Christ our Lord.

The word concerning "your seed" and "My son" [in 2 Samuel
7:12-14a] indicates that the seed of David would become the Son
of God, that the seed of a man would become God's Son.

This thought is continued very strongly in the New Testament,
particularly in Romans 1:3 and 4....Here we have the same thought
as in 2 Samuel 7:12-14a—that the seed of David becomes the Son
of God. These verses reveal, on the one hand, that Christ is the
seed of David and, on the other hand, that He, the seed of David,
has been designated the Son of God. When we compare these two
portions of the Word, we see that both in the Old Testament and
in the New Testament we have the matter of the seed of David
becoming the Son of God. (*Life-study of 1 & 2 Samuel,* p. 165)

Today's Reading

In 2 Samuel 7 we see that David had a good heart toward God
and wanted to build a house for God. However, God intervened
and did not permit David to do this, because David did not have
an adequate and thorough view of God's economy. After stopping
David from building Him a house, God went on to reveal something further concerning His economy. In this chapter, therefore,
the divine revelation took a great step forward.

The Bible tells us that David was a man according to God's
heart (1 Sam. 13:14)....Yes, David was a man according to the
heart of God, but...he was still a man in life, in nature, and in constitution;...he was not God in life and in nature. David could not

say, "To me, to live is Christ" or "It is no longer I who live, but it is Christ who lives in me" (Phil. 1:21a; Gal. 2:20).

This brings us to the matter of deification—God's intention to make the believers God in life and in nature but not in the Godhead. Athanasius referred to deification when at the council of Nicea in A.D. 325 he said, "He [Christ] was made man that we might be made God."

I have learned from my study of the Bible that God does intend to make the believers God in life and in nature but not in the Godhead. For instance, 1 John 3:2 says, "Beloved, now we are children of God, and it has not yet been manifested what we will be. We know that if He is manifested, we will be like Him because we will see Him even as He is." This verse clearly reveals that we will be like God.

God makes us like Him by imparting His life and nature into us. Second Peter 1:4 says that we have become "partakers of the divine nature." John 1:12-13 says that we were born, regenerated, by God with His life. As God's children we are "baby gods," having God's life and nature but not His Godhead. The Godhead is unique; He is the only One who should be worshipped.

We have been born of God and today, having God's life and nature, we are partially like Him. One day, when He comes, we will be wholly and entirely like Him.

It was wonderful for David to be a man according to God's heart, but it was not sufficient. God wants those who can say, "I am not just a person according to God's heart. I am God in life and in nature but not in His Godhead." On the one hand, the New Testament reveals that the Godhead is unique and that only God, who alone has the Godhead, should be worshipped. On the other hand, the New Testament reveals that we, the believers in Christ, have God's life and nature and that we are becoming God in life and in nature but will never have His Godhead. (*Life-study of 1 & 2 Samuel,* pp. 166-167)

Further Reading: Life-study of 1 & 2 Samuel, msg. 27; *Life-study of Romans,* msgs. 52-54

Enlightenment and inspiration: _____

_____

_____

_____

Morning Nourishment

Heb. **For to which of the angels has He ever said, "You**
1:5 **are My Son; this day have I begotten You"?...**
John **...If anyone loves Me, he will keep My word, and**
14:23 **My Father will love him, and We will come to him**
and make an abode with him.

David had the heart to build a house for God, but God indicated to David that this was neither what he needed nor what God needed. God told David that He would build One to be David's seed and that this seed would be called God's Son. This seed would be both divine and human. Hebrews 1:5 indicates that this refers to Christ as God's firstborn Son. Furthermore, as we have seen, Romans 1:3-4, which corresponds to 2 Samuel 7:12-14a, tells us that in resurrection the seed of David was designated the Son of God. In their intrinsic significance, 2 Samuel 7:12-14a and Romans 1:3-4 reveal to us a human and divine person. (*Life-study of 1 & 2 Samuel,* p. 167)

Today's Reading

Just as the photograph of a person does not have the life and nature of that person, so David, a photograph of God's heart, did not have the life and nature of God. Even though he was a man whose heart was according to God, he did not have anything related to God organically. What David needed is what we need today. We need God to build Himself in Christ into our humanity. This means that we need God to work Himself in Christ into us as our life, our nature, and our constitution. As a result,...we can declare that we have God's life, nature, and constitution.

In order to accomplish this, God in Christ became a man and went through some processes that this man could be designated something divine. In resurrection He was designated the firstborn Son of God. In and through resurrection Christ, the firstborn Son of God, became the life-giving Spirit, who now enters into us to impart, to dispense, Himself as life into our being to be our inner constitution, to make us a God-man just like Him. He was God becoming man, and we are man becoming God in life and in nature but not in the Godhead.

Many Christians are still trying merely to have a behaving, a living, and a being that are according to God's heart, but they do not have the concept that God desires to build Himself in Christ into our being. What He is building into us will be His abode, which will be our abode also. Hence, it becomes a mutual abode. The New Jerusalem is this mutual abode. On the one hand, the New Jerusalem is the dwelling place of God; on the other hand, it is also our eternal dwelling place (Rev. 21:3, 22). For eternity the New Jerusalem will be the fulfillment of the Lord's brief word in John 15:4: "Abide in Me and I in you."

David wanted to build God a house of cedar, but God wanted to build Himself in Christ into David. What God would build into David would be both God's house and David's house. This mutual abode is also unveiled in John 14:23. [The] abode [in this verse] will be...both God's habitation and our habitation.

We need to realize that God will have a habitation not by our doing or working but by His building. Christ builds the church (Matt. 16:18) by coming into our spirit and spreading Himself from our spirit into our mind, emotion, and will to occupy our entire soul. This church will become His habitation and our habitation. This is what we need, and our burden is to emphasize this one thing.

There is no need for us to build anything for God. Rather, God needs to build Himself in Christ into us as our life, nature, and essence. Eventually, the Triune God will become our intrinsic constitution. We will be constituted with the Triune God. That will be the seed of David and the Son of God—something divine and human satisfying God's need and our need for a mutual abode. The New Jerusalem is the consummation of this mutual abode, and we will all be there. (*Life-study of 1 & 2 Samuel*, pp. 168-169)

Further Reading: Life-study of 1 & 2 Samuel, msgs. 25-26; Watchman Nee: A Seer of the Divine Revelation in the Present Age, chs. 15-16; The Organic Building Up of the Church as the Body of Christ to be the Organism of the Processed and Dispensing Triune God, ch. 2

Enlightenment and inspiration: _____

_____

_____

Morning Nourishment

2 Sam. ...I will raise up your seed after you....I will be his
7:12, 14 Father, and he will be My son....
Matt. Saying, What do you think concerning the Christ?
22:42-43 Whose son is He? They said to Him, David's. He said to
them, How then does David in spirit call Him Lord...
45 If then David calls Him Lord, how is He his son?

In 2 Samuel 7:12 God speaks of David's seed, and in verse 14a
He says, "I will be his Father, and he will be My son." Here we
have something of very great significance—the seed of David becoming the Son of God. These verses clearly unveil that a seed of
man, that is, a son of a man, can become the Son of God. This im-
plies that God's intention is to make Himself man in order to
make man God in life and in nature but not in the Godhead. Such
an implication is exceedingly great. Eventually, the whole Bible
consummates with this matter. The New Jerusalem, the ultimate
consummation of the Bible, involves God becoming man and man
becoming God in life and in nature but not in the Godhead and
God and man being mingled together to be one entity. (Life-study
of 1 & 2 Samuel, p. 203)

Today's Reading

If we read the Bible without paying attention to this crucial
point, then, in a very real sense, the Bible is to us an empty book.
This means that although the Bible is real in itself, in our understanding of it the Bible is empty. As an illustration, let us suppose
that a certain box, which is quite attractive, contains a large diamond. A child may be interested in the box but not in the diamond.
An adult, however, would focus his attention on the diamond con-
tained in the box. Today, many Christians care for the Bible as the
"box," but they have not seen and do not appreciate the "diamond,"
which is the content of this box, and they may even condemn those
who have a proper appreciation of the "diamond" in the "box." The
"diamond" in the "box" of the Bible is the revelation that in Christ
God has become man in order that man might become God in life
and in nature but not in the Godhead.

The vast majority of today's Christians neglect the crucial point in the Bible that in Christ God has become man in order to make man God in life and in nature but not in the Godhead and that God desires to mingle Himself with man to be one entity. Some not only neglect this; they falsely accuse as heretical those who teach it. Today many believe one aspect of this crucial point—that God became a man named Jesus—but they do not believe the other aspect—that man is becoming God in life and in nature but not in the Godhead.

The Bible reveals a wonderful, marvelous person—Jesus Christ, the God-man. This One is both the Son of God and the Son of man. On one occasion when the Pharisees were gathered together, the Lord Jesus questioned them, saying, "What do you think concerning the Christ? Whose son is He?" (Matt. 22:41-42a). When they said to him "David's," He went on to say to them, "How then does David in spirit call Him Lord?…If then David calls Him Lord, how is He his son?" (vv. 43, 45)….Here the Lord Jesus was indicating that He, the son of David, was the Son of God—the very matter revealed in 2 Samuel 7:12-14a.

What is revealed in 2 Samuel 7 is expounded by Paul in Romans 1:3-4, where he tells us that Christ, a descendant of David, has been designated the Son of God. These verses say, "Concerning His Son, who came out of the seed of David according to the flesh, who was designated the Son of God…out of the resurrection of the dead, Jesus Christ our Lord." Christ is a descendant of David, yet He has been designated to be the Son of God. This is the mystery of God becoming man to make man God in life and in nature but not in the Godhead. The two, God and man, are thus built together, constituted into each other. In Christ God has been constituted into man, man has been constituted into God, and God and man have been mingled together to be one entity, which is called the God-man. (*Life-study of 1 & 2 Samuel,* pp. 204-205)

Further Reading: Life-study of 1 & 2 Samuel, msgs. 28-29, 31; *Life-study of Romans,* msgs. 55-56

Enlightenment and inspiration: _____

_____

_____

_____

Morning Nourishment

Rev. And I saw the holy city, New Jerusalem, coming down
21:2 out of heaven from God, prepared as a bride adorned
for her husband.
11 Having the glory of God. Her light was like a most
precious stone, like a jasper stone, as clear as crystal.
18-19 ...And the city was pure gold, like clear glass. The
foundations of the wall of the city were adorned with
every precious stone...
21 And the twelve gates were twelve pearls...

In these messages on 2 Samuel 7, we have emphasized the
matter of God's building Himself in Christ into man. God is building Himself not in Himself but in man, and not only *in* man but
also *into* man. This building is God's constituting of Himself in
Christ into man.

God in Christ is constituting Himself into man, making Himself the element of man. Thus, we human beings are constituted
with a divine element. This means that a divine element is built
into our human element, and the two elements are mingled with
each other. Not only is God's divine element constituted into us—
the human element is constituted into God. As the divine element
is constituted into our humanity, we become God in life and in nature but not in the Godhead. As the human element is constituted
into God, God becomes man. This is the building revealed in the
New Testament. (*Life-study of 1 & 2 Samuel,* p. 205)

Today's Reading

Such a revelation should become a principle that governs
our understanding of God and of God's building. When we talk
about the building up of the church or about the building up of
the Body, we need to realize that this building is a constitution
of the divine element into the human element and of the human
element into the divine element. This building, therefore, is a
constitution of the divine element and of the human element into
each other. Such a constitution makes the divine element and
the human element one entity. This is the building of the church,

the building of the Body of Christ.

As we work for God today, we should participate in this building. This means that our work must be part of this mutual constitution. If our work is not related to this mutual constitution, then in the eyes of God our work is like wood, grass, and stubble (1 Cor. 3:12). But if our work is a part of this mutual constitution, God will regard our work as gold, silver, and precious stones, which will consummate in the New Jerusalem built with gold, pearl, and precious stones (Rev. 21:2, 11, 18-21).

The conclusion of the divine revelation in the Bible is a building, the New Jerusalem. This building is a blending and mingling of divinity with humanity....Revelation 21:3 refers to the New Jerusalem as "the tabernacle of God," and verse 22 says, "...The Lord God the Almighty and the Lamb are its temple." The New Jerusalem as the tabernacle of God is for God to dwell in, and God and the Lamb as the temple are for the redeemed saints to dwell in. This indicates that the New Jerusalem will be a mutual dwelling place for God and man. Furthermore, this building is a composition of human beings. The gates are pearls inscribed with the names of the twelve tribes of the sons of Israel (v. 12), and on the twelve foundations are the twelve names of the twelve apostles of the Lamb (v. 14). This indicates clearly that the New Jerusalem is a composition of the Triune God, who is the essence, center, and universality, and God's redeemed people.

The New Jerusalem is a composition of divinity and humanity blended and mingled together as one entity. All the components have the same life, nature, and constitution and thus are a corporate person. This is a matter of God becoming man and man becoming God in life and in nature but not in the Godhead. These two, God and man, man and God, are built up together by being blended and mingled together. This is the completion, the consummation, of God's building. We all need to see this vision. (*Life-study of 1 & 2 Samuel,* pp. 206-207, 198-199)

Further Reading: Life-study of 1 & 2 Samuel, msgs. 30-31

Enlightenment and inspiration: _____
_____
_____
_____

What Miracle! What Mystery!

1   What miracle! What mystery!
     That God and man should blended be!
     God became man to make man God,
     Untraceable economy!
     From His good pleasure, heart's desire,
     His highest goal attained will be.
     From His good pleasure, heart's desire,
     His highest goal attained will be.

2   Flesh He became, the first God-man,
     His pleasure that I God may be:
     In life and nature I'm God's kind,
     Though Godhead's His exclusively.
     His attributes my virtues are;
     His glorious image shines through me.
     His attributes my virtues are;
     His glorious image shines through me.

3   No longer I alone that live,
     But God together lives with me.
     Built with the saints in the Triune God,
     His universal house we'll be,
     And His organic Body we
     For His expression corp'rately.
     And His organic Body we
     For His expression corp'rately.

4   Jerusalem, the ultimate,
     Of visions the totality;
     The Triune God, tripartite man—
     A loving pair eternally—
     As man yet God they coinhere,
     A mutual dwelling place to be;
     God's glory in humanity
     Shines forth in splendor radiantly!

Composition for prophecy with main point and sub-points: _____

_____

_____

_____

_____

_____

_____

_____

_____

_____

_____

_____

_____

_____

_____

_____

_____

_____

_____

_____

_____

_____

_____

_____

_____

_____

_____

_____

_____

_____

_____

_____

_____

_____

_____

_____

Reading Schedule for the Recovery Version of the New Testament with Footnotes

Wk.	Lord's Day	Monday	Tuesday	Wednesday	Thursday	Friday	Saturday
1	☐ Matt 1:1-2	☐ 1:3-7	☐ 1:8-17	☐ 1:18-25	☐ 2:1-23	☐ 3:1-6	☐ 3:7-17
2	☐ 4:1-11	☐ 4:12-25	☐ 5:1-4	☐ 5:5-12	☐ 5:13-20	☐ 5:21-26	☐ 5:27-48
3	☐ 6:1-8	☐ 6:9-18	☐ 6:19-34	☐ 7:1-12	☐ 7:13-29	☐ 8:1-13	☐ 8:14-22
4	☐ 8:23-34	☐ 9:1-13	☐ 9:14-17	☐ 9:18-34	☐ 9:35—10:5	☐ 10:6-25	☐ 10:26-42
5	☐ 11:1-15	☐ 11:16-30	☐ 12:1-14	☐ 12:15-32	☐ 12:33-42	☐ 12:43—13:2	☐ 13:3-12
6	☐ 13:13-30	☐ 13:31-43	☐ 13:44-58	☐ 14:1-13	☐ 14:14-21	☐ 14:22-36	☐ 15:1-20
7	☐ 15:21-31	☐ 15:32-39	☐ 16:1-12	☐ 16:13-20	☐ 16:21-28	☐ 17:1-13	☐ 17:14-27
8	☐ 18:1-14	☐ 18:15-22	☐ 18:23-35	☐ 19:1-15	☐ 19:16-30	☐ 20:1-16	☐ 20:17-34
9	☐ 21:1-11	☐ 21:12-22	☐ 21:23-32	☐ 21:33-46	☐ 22:1-22	☐ 22:23-33	☐ 22:34-46
10	☐ 23:1-12	☐ 23:13-39	☐ 24:1-14	☐ 24:15-31	☐ 24:32-51	☐ 25:1-13	☐ 25:14-30
11	☐ 25:31-46	☐ 26:1-16	☐ 26:17-35	☐ 26:36-46	☐ 26:47-64	☐ 26:65-75	☐ 27:1-26
12	☐ 27:27-44	☐ 27:45-56	☐ 27:57—28:15	☐ 28:16-20	☐ Mark 1:1	☐ 1:2-6	☐ 1:7-13
13	☐ 1:14-28	☐ 1:29-45	☐ 2:1-12	☐ 2:13-28	☐ 3:1-19	☐ 3:20-35	☐ 4:1-25
14	☐ 4:26-41	☐ 5:1-20	☐ 5:21-43	☐ 6:1-29	☐ 6:30-56	☐ 7:1-23	☐ 7:24-37
15	☐ 8:1-26	☐ 8:27—9:1	☐ 9:2-29	☐ 9:30-50	☐ 10:1-16	☐ 10:17-34	☐ 10:35-52
16	☐ 11:1-16	☐ 11:17-33	☐ 12:1-27	☐ 12:28-44	☐ 13:1-13	☐ 13:14-37	☐ 14:1-26
17	☐ 14:27-52	☐ 14:53-72	☐ 15:1-15	☐ 15:16-47	☐ 16:1-8	☐ 16:9-20	☐ Luke 1:1-4
18	☐ 1:5-25	☐ 1:26-46	☐ 1:47-56	☐ 1:57-80	☐ 2:1-8	☐ 2:9-20	☐ 2:21-39
19	☐ 2:40-52	☐ 3:1-20	☐ 3:21-38	☐ 4:1-13	☐ 4:14-30	☐ 4:31-44	☐ 5:1-26
20	☐ 5:27—6:16	☐ 6:17-38	☐ 6:39-49	☐ 7:1-17	☐ 7:18-23	☐ 7:24-35	☐ 7:36-50
21	☐ 8:1-15	☐ 8:16-25	☐ 8:26-39	☐ 8:40-56	☐ 9:1-17	☐ 9:18-26	☐ 9:27-36
22	☐ 9:37-50	☐ 9:51-62	☐ 10:1-11	☐ 10:12-24	☐ 10:25-37	☐ 10:38-42	☐ 11:1-13
23	☐ 11:14-26	☐ 11:27-36	☐ 11:37-54	☐ 12:1-12	☐ 12:13-21	☐ 12:22-34	☐ 12:35-48
24	☐ 12:49-59	☐ 13:1-9	☐ 13:10-17	☐ 13:18-30	☐ 13:31—14:6	☐ 14:7-14	☐ 14:15-24
25	☐ 14:25-35	☐ 15:1-10	☐ 15:11-21	☐ 15:22-32	☐ 16:1-13	☐ 16:14-22	☐ 16:23-31
26	☐ 17:1-19	☐ 17:20-37	☐ 18:1-14	☐ 18:15-30	☐ 18:31-43	☐ 19:1-10	☐ 19:11-27

Reading Schedule for the Recovery Version of the New Testament with Footnotes

Wk.	Lord's Day	Monday	Tuesday	Wednesday	Thursday	Friday	Saturday
27	□ Luke 19:28-48	□ 20:1-19	□ 20:20-38	□ 20:39—21:4	□ 21:5-27	□ 21:28-38	□ 22:1-20
28	□ 22:21-38	□ 22:39-54	□ 22:55-71	□ 23:1-43	□ 23:44-56	□ 24:1-12	□ 24:13-35
29	□ 24:36-53	□ John 1:1-13	□ 1:14-18	□ 1:19-34	□ 1:35-51	□ 2:1-11	□ 2:12-22
30	□ 2:23—3:13	□ 3:14-21	□ 3:22-36	□ 4:1-14	□ 4:15-26	□ 4:27-42	□ 4:43-54
31	□ 5:1-16	□ 5:17-30	□ 5:31-47	□ 6:1-15	□ 6:16-31	□ 6:32-51	□ 6:52-71
32	□ 7:1-9	□ 7:10-24	□ 7:25-36	□ 7:37-52	□ 7:53—8:11	□ 8:12-27	□ 8:28-44
33	□ 8:45-59	□ 9:1-13	□ 9:14-34	□ 9:35—10:9	□ 10:10-30	□ 10:31—11:4	□ 11:5-22
34	□ 11:23-40	□ 11:41-57	□ 12:1-11	□ 12:12-24	□ 12:25-36	□ 12:37-50	□ 13:1-11
35	□ 13:12-30	□ 13:31-38	□ 14:1-6	□ 14:7-20	□ 14:21-31	□ 15:1-11	□ 15:12-27
36	□ 16:1-15	□ 16:16-33	□ 17:1-5	□ 17:6-13	□ 17:14-24	□ 17:25—18:11	□ 18:12-27
37	□ 18:28-40	□ 19:1-16	□ 19:17-30	□ 19:31-42	□ 20:1-13	□ 20:14-18	□ 20:19-22
38	□ 20:23-31	□ 21:1-14	□ 21:15-22	□ 21:23-25	□ Acts 1:1-8	□ 1:9-14	□ 1:15-26
39	□ 2:1-13	□ 2:14-21	□ 2:22-36	□ 2:37-41	□ 2:42-47	□ 3:1-18	□ 3:19—4:22
40	□ 4:23-37	□ 5:1-16	□ 5:17-32	□ 5:33-42	□ 6:1—7:1	□ 7:2-29	□ 7:30-60
41	□ 8:1-13	□ 8:14-25	□ 8:26-40	□ 9:1-19	□ 9:20-43	□ 10:1-16	□ 10:17-33
42	□ 10:34-48	□ 11:1-18	□ 11:19-30	□ 12:1-25	□ 13:1-12	□ 13:13-43	□ 13:44—14:5
43	□ 14:6-28	□ 15:1-12	□ 15:13-34	□ 15:35—16:5	□ 16:6-18	□ 16:19-40	□ 17:1-18
44	□ 17:19-34	□ 18:1-17	□ 18:18-28	□ 19:1-20	□ 19:21-41	□ 20:1-12	□ 20:13-38
45	□ 21:1-14	□ 21:15-26	□ 21:27-40	□ 22:1-21	□ 22:22-29	□ 22:30—23:11	□ 23:12-15
46	□ 23:16-30	□ 23:31—24:21	□ 24:22—25:5	□ 25:6-27	□ 26:1-13	□ 26:14-32	□ 27:1-26
47	□ 27:27—28:10	□ 28:11-22	□ 28:23-31	□ Rom 1:1-2	□ 1:3-7	□ 1:8-17	□ 1:18-25
48	□ 1:26—2:10	□ 2:11-29	□ 3:1-20	□ 3:21-31	□ 4:1-12	□ 4:13-25	□ 5:1-11
49	□ 5:12-17	□ 5:18—6:5	□ 6:6-11	□ 6:12-23	□ 7:1-12	□ 7:13-25	□ 8:1-2
50	□ 8:3-6	□ 8:7-13	□ 8:14-25	□ 8:26-39	□ 9:1-18	□ 9:19—10:3	□ 10:4-15
51	□ 10:16—11:10	□ 11:11-22	□ 11:23-36	□ 12:1-3	□ 12:4-21	□ 13:1-14	□ 14:1-12
52	□ 14:13-23	□ 15:1-13	□ 15:14-33	□ 16:1-5	□ 16:6-24	□ 16:25-27	□ I Cor 1:1-4

Reading Schedule for the Recovery Version of the New Testament with Footnotes

Wk.	Lord's Day	Monday	Tuesday	Wednesday	Thursday	Friday	Saturday
53	☐ I Cor 1:5-9	☐ 1:10-17	☐ 1:18-31	☐ 2:1-5	☐ 2:6-10	☐ 2:11-16	☐ 3:1-9
54	☐ 3:10-13	☐ 3:14-23	☐ 4:1-9	☐ 4:10-21	☐ 5:1-13	☐ 6:1-11	☐ 6:12-20
55	☐ 7:1-16	☐ 7:17-24	☐ 7:25-40	☐ 8:1-13	☐ 9:1-15	☐ 9:16-27	☐ 10:1-4
56	☐ 10:5-13	☐ 10:14-33	☐ 11:1-6	☐ 11:7-16	☐ 11:17-26	☐ 11:27-34	☐ 12:1-11
57	☐ 12:12-22	☐ 12:23-31	☐ 13:1-13	☐ 14:1-12	☐ 14:13-25	☐ 14:26-33	☐ 14:34-40
58	☐ 15:1-19	☐ 15:20-28	☐ 15:29-34	☐ 15:35-49	☐ 15:50-58	☐ 16:1-9	☐ 16:10-24
59	☐ II Cor 1:1-4	☐ 1:5-14	☐ 1:15-22	☐ 1:23—2:11	☐ 2:12-17	☐ 3:1-6	☐ 3:7-11
60	☐ 3:12-18	☐ 4:1-6	☐ 4:7-12	☐ 4:13-18	☐ 5:1-8	☐ 5:9-15	☐ 5:16-21
61	☐ 6:1-13	☐ 6:14—7:4	☐ 7:5-16	☐ 8:1-15	☐ 8:16-24	☐ 9:1-15	☐ 10:1-6
62	☐ 10:7-18	☐ 11:1-15	☐ 11:16-33	☐ 12:1-10	☐ 12:11-21	☐ 13:1-10	☐ 13:11-14
63	☐ Gal 1:1-5	☐ 1:6-14	☐ 1:15-24	☐ 2:1-13	☐ 2:14-21	☐ 3:1-4	☐ 3:5-14
64	☐ 3:15-22	☐ 3:23-29	☐ 4:1-7	☐ 4:8-20	☐ 4:21-31	☐ 5:1-12	☐ 5:13-21
65	☐ 5:22-26	☐ 6:1-10	☐ 6:11-15	☐ 6:16-18	☐ Eph 1:1-3	☐ 1:4-6	☐ 1:7-10
66	☐ 1:11-14	☐ 1:15-18	☐ 1:19-23	☐ 2:1-5	☐ 2:6-10	☐ 2:11-14	☐ 2:15-18
67	☐ 2:19-22	☐ 3:1-7	☐ 3:8-13	☐ 3:14-18	☐ 3:19-21	☐ 4:1-4	☐ 4:5-10
68	☐ 4:11-16	☐ 4:17-24	☐ 4:25-32	☐ 5:1-10	☐ 5:11-21	☐ 5:22-26	☐ 5:27-33
69	☐ 6:1-9	☐ 6:10-14	☐ 6:15-18	☐ 6:19-24	☐ Phil 1:1-7	☐ 1:8-18	☐ 1:19-26
70	☐ 1:27—2:4	☐ 2:5-11	☐ 2:12-16	☐ 2:17-30	☐ 3:1-6	☐ 3:7-11	☐ 3:12-16
71	☐ 3:17-21	☐ 4:1-9	☐ 4:10-23	☐ Col 1:1-8	☐ 1:9-13	☐ 1:14-23	☐ 1:24-29
72	☐ 2:1-7	☐ 2:8-15	☐ 2:16-23	☐ 3:1-4	☐ 3:5-15	☐ 3:16-25	☐ 4:1-18
73	☐ I Thes 1:1-3	☐ 1:4-10	☐ 2:1-12	☐ 2:13—3:5	☐ 3:6-13	☐ 4:1-10	☐ 4:11—5:11
74	☐ 5:12-28	☐ II Thes 1:1-12	☐ 2:1-17	☐ 3:1-18	☐ I Tim 1:1-2	☐ 1:3-4	☐ 1:5-14
75	☐ 1:15-20	☐ 2:1-7	☐ 2:8-15	☐ 3:1-13	☐ 3:14—4:5	☐ 4:6-16	☐ 5:1-25
76	☐ 6:1-10	☐ 6:11-21	☐ II Tim 1:1-10	☐ 1:11-18	☐ 2:1-15	☐ 2:16-26	☐ 3:1-13
77	☐ 3:14—4:8	☐ 4:9-22	☐ Titus 1:1-4	☐ 1:5-16	☐ 2:1-15	☐ 3:1-8	☐ 3:9-15
78	☐ Philem 1:1-11	☐ 1:12-25	☐ Heb 1:1-2	☐ 1:3-5	☐ 1:6-14	☐ 2:1-9	☐ 2:10-18

Reading Schedule for the Recovery Version of the New Testament with Footnotes

Wk.	Lord's Day	Monday	Tuesday	Wednesday	Thursday	Friday	Saturday
79	☐ Heb 3:1-6	☐ 3:7-19	☐ 4:1-9	☐ 4:10-13	☐ 4:14-16	☐ 5:1-10	☐ 5:11—6:3
80	☐ 6:4-8	☐ 6:9-20	☐ 7:1-10	☐ 7:11-28	☐ 8:1-6	☐ 8:7-13	☐ 9:1-4
81	☐ 9:5-14	☐ 9:15-28	☐ 10:1-18	☐ 10:19-28	☐ 10:29-39	☐ 11:1-6	☐ 11:7-19
82	☐ 11:20-31	☐ 11:32-40	☐ 12:1-2	☐ 12:3-13	☐ 12:14-17	☐ 12:18-26	☐ 12:27-29
83	☐ 13:1-7	☐ 13:8-12	☐ 13:13-15	☐ 13:16-25	☐ James1:1-8	☐ 1:9-18	☐ 1:19-27
84	☐ 2:1-13	☐ 2:14-26	☐ 3:1-18	☐ 4:1-10	☐ 4:11-17	☐ 5:1-12	☐ 5:13-20
85	☐ I Pet 1:1-2	☐ 1:3-4	☐ 1:5	☐ 1:6-9	☐ 1:10-12	☐ 1:13-17	☐ 1:18-25
86	☐ 2:1-3	☐ 2:4-8	☐ 2:9-17	☐ 2:18-25	☐ 3:1-13	☐ 3:14-22	☐ 4:1-6
87	☐ 4:7-16	☐ 4:17-19	☐ 5:1-4	☐ 5:5-9	☐ 5:10-14	☐ II Pet 1:1-2	☐ 1:3-4
88	☐ 1:5-8	☐ 1:9-11	☐ 1:12-18	☐ 1:19-21	☐ 2:1-3	☐ 2:4-11	☐ 2:12-22
89	☐ 3:1-6	☐ 3:7-9	☐ 3:10-12	☐ 3:13-15	☐ 3:16	☐ 3:17-18	☐ I John 1:1-2
90	☐ 1:3-4	☐ 1:5	☐ 1:6	☐ 1:7	☐ 1:8-10	☐ 2:1-2	☐ 2:3-11
91	☐ 2:12-14	☐ 2:15-19	☐ 2:20-23	☐ 2:24-27	☐ 2:28-29	☐ 3:1-5	☐ 3:6-10
92	☐ 3:11-18	☐ 3:19-24	☐ 4:1-6	☐ 4:7-11	☐ 4:12-15	☐ 4:16—5:3	☐ 5:4-13
93	☐ 5:14-17	☐ 5:18-21	☐ II John 1:1-3	☐ 1:4-9	☐ 1:10-13	☐ III John 1:1-6	☐ 1:7-14
94	☐ Jude 1:1-4	☐ 1:5-10	☐ 1:11-19	☐ 1:20-25	☐ Rev 1:1-3	☐ 1:4-6	☐ 1:7-11
95	☐ 1:12-13	☐ 1:14-16	☐ 1:17-20	☐ 2:1-6	☐ 2:7	☐ 2:8-9	☐ 2:10-11
96	☐ 2:12-14	☐ 2:15-17	☐ 2:18-23	☐ 2:24-29	☐ 3:1-3	☐ 3:4-6	☐ 3:7-9
97	☐ 3:10-13	☐ 3:14-18	☐ 3:19-22	☐ 4:1-5	☐ 4:6-7	☐ 4:8-11	☐ 5:1-6
98	☐ 5:7-14	☐ 6:1-8	☐ 6:9-17	☐ 7:1-8	☐ 7:9-17	☐ 8:1-6	☐ 8:7-12
99	☐ 8:13—9:11	☐ 9:12-21	☐ 10:1-4	☐ 10:5-11	☐ 11:1-4	☐ 11:5-14	☐ 11:15-19
100	☐ 12:1-4	☐ 12:5-9	☐ 12:10-18	☐ 13:1-10	☐ 13:11-18	☐ 14:1-5	☐ 14:6-12
101	☐ 14:13-20	☐ 15:1-8	☐ 16:1-12	☐ 16:13-21	☐ 17:1-6	☐ 17:7-18	☐ 18:1-8
102	☐ 18:9—19:4	☐ 19:5-10	☐ 19:11-16	☐ 19:17-21	☐ 20:1-6	☐ 20:7-10	☐ 20:11-15
103	☐ 21:1	☐ 21:2	☐ 21:3-8	☐ 21:9-13	☐ 21:14-18	☐ 21:19-21	☐ 21:22-27
104	☐ 22:1	☐ 22:2	☐ 22:3-11	☐ 22:12-15	☐ 22:16-17	☐ 22:18-21	☐

Week 7 — Day 1 — Today's verses

Matt. And Simon Peter answered and said, You
16:16 are the Christ, the Son of the living God.
18 And I...say to you that you are Peter, and upon this rock I will build My church...

1 Cor. For another foundation no one is able to
3:11 lay besides that which is laid, which is Jesus Christ.

1:2 To the church of God which is in Corinth, to those who have been sanctified in Christ Jesus...

_____
Date

Week 7 — Day 2 — Today's verses

1 Cor. According to the grace of God given to
3:10 me, as a wise master builder I have laid a foundation, and another builds upon *it*. But let each man take heed how he builds upon *it*.

12 But if anyone builds upon the foundation gold, silver, precious stones, wood, grass, stubble.

_____
Date

Week 7 — Day 3 — Today's verses

Eph. Being built upon the foundation of the
2:20 apostles and prophets, Christ Jesus Himself being the cornerstone.

3:4-5 ...You can perceive my understanding in the mystery of Christ, which in other generations was not made known to the sons of men, as it has now been revealed to His holy apostles and prophets in spirit.

_____
Date

Week 7 — Day 4 — Today's verses

Eph. Being diligent to keep the oneness of the
4:3-4 Spirit in the uniting bond of peace: one Body and one Spirit, even as also you were called in one hope of your calling.

John That they all may be one; even as You,
17:21-23 Father, are in Me and I in You, that they also may be in Us; that the world may believe that You have sent Me. And the glory which You have given Me I have given to them, that they may be one, even as We are one; I in them, and You in Me, that they may be perfected into one...

_____
Date

Week 7 — Day 5 — Today's verses

Deut. But to the place which Jehovah your God
12:5 will choose out of all your tribes to put His name, to His habitation, shall you seek, and there shall you go.

11 Then to the place where Jehovah your God will choose to cause His name to dwell, there you shall bring all that I am commanding you, your burnt offerings and your sacrifices, your tithes and the heave offering of your hand and all your choice vows which you vow to Jehovah.

Eph. In whom you also are being built together
2:22 into a dwelling place of God in spirit.

_____
Date

Week 7 — Day 6 — Today's verses

Matt. And he who does not take his cross and
10:38 follow after Me is not worthy of Me.

1 Cor. For I did not determine to know anything
2:2 among you except Jesus Christ, and this One crucified.

Gal. But far be it from me to boast except in the
6:14 cross of our Lord Jesus Christ, through whom the world has been crucified to me and I to the world.

_____
Date

Week 8 — Day 4   **Today's verses**

Matt. 13:46 And finding one pearl of great value, he went and sold all that he had and bought it.

Rev. 21:21 ...The twelve gates were twelve pearls; each one of the gates was, respectively, of one pearl. And the street of the city was pure gold, like transparent glass.

18 And the building work of its wall was jasper...

Date

Week 8 — Day 5   **Today's verses**

1 Cor. 3:9 For we are God's fellow workers; you are God's cultivated land, God's building.

12 But if anyone builds upon the foundation gold, silver, precious stones...

Date

Week 8 — Day 6   **Today's verses**

1 Cor. 3:12-13 But if anyone builds upon the foundation gold, silver, precious stones, wood, grass, stubble, the work of each will become manifest; for the day will declare *it*, because it is revealed by fire, and the fire itself will prove each one's work, of what sort it is.

1 Pet. 1:24 For "all flesh is like grass, and all its glory like the flower of grass. The grass has withered, and the flower has fallen off."

Date

Week 8 — Day 1   **Today's verses**

Gen. 2:10-12 And a river went forth from Eden to water the garden, and from there it divided and became four branches. The name of the first is Pishon; it is the one that goes around the whole land of Havilah, where there is gold. And the gold of that land is good; bdellium and onyx stone are there.

Rev. 21:18-19 And the building work of its wall was jasper; and the city was pure gold, like clear glass. The foundations of the wall of the city were adorned with every precious stone: the first foundation was jasper...

21 And the twelve gates were twelve pearls...

Date

Week 8 — Day 2   **Today's verses**

1 Cor. 3:10-12 According to the grace of God given to me, as a wise master builder I have laid a foundation, and another builds upon *it*. But let each man take heed how he builds upon *it*. For another foundation no one is able to lay besides that which is laid, which is Jesus Christ. But if anyone builds upon the foundation gold, silver, precious stones, wood, grass, stubble.

Exo. 28:17 And you shall enclose in [the breastplate] enclosures of stones, four rows of stones...

21 And the stones shall be according to the names of the sons of Israel,...*like* the engravings of a signet...for the twelve tribes.

Date

Week 8 — Day 3   **Today's verses**

1 Cor. 3:12 But if anyone builds upon the foundation gold, silver, precious stones, wood, grass, stubble.

2 Pet. 1:4 Through which He has granted to us precious and exceedingly great promises that through these you might become partakers of the divine nature...

Date

Week 9 — Day 4　　Today's verses

Eph. In whom all the building, being fitted to-
2:21-22 gether, is growing into a holy temple in the Lord; in whom you also are being built together into a dwelling place of God in spirit.

Eph. But holding to truth in love, we may grow
4:15-16 up into Him in all things, who is the Head, Christ, out from whom all the Body, being joined together and being knit together,… causes the growth of the Body unto the building up of itself in love.

1 Cor. But if anyone builds upon the foundation
3:12-13 gold, silver, precious stones, wood, grass, stubble, the work of each will become manifest; for the day will declare it, because it will be revealed by fire,…of what sort it is.

_____
Date

Week 9 — Day 5　　Today's verses

1 Cor. The work of each will become mani-
3:13-17 fest,…because it is revealed by fire, and the fire itself will prove each one's work, of what sort it is. If anyone's work which he has built upon the foundation remains, he will receive a reward; if anyone's work is consumed, he will suffer loss.…Do you not know that you are the temple of God, and that the Spirit of God dwells in you? If anyone destroys the temple of God, God will destroy him…

_____
Date

Week 9 — Day 6　　Today's verses

Eph. According to the eternal purpose which
3:11 He made in Christ Jesus our Lord.

Rom. Because out from Him and through Him
11:36 and to Him are all things. To Him be the glory forever. Amen.

_____
Date

Week 9 — Day 1　　Today's verses

Eph. That you put off…the old man,…and that
4:22-23 you be renewed in the spirit of your mind.

Rom. And do not be fashioned according to this
12:2 age, but be transformed by the renewing of the mind that you may prove what the will of God is, that which is good and well pleasing and perfect.

2 Cor. But we all with unveiled face, beholding
3:18 and reflecting like a mirror the glory of the Lord, are being transformed into the same image from glory to glory, even as from the Lord Spirit.

_____
Date

Week 9 — Day 2　　Today's verses

Exo. And you shall make the boards for the
26:15 tabernacle of acacia wood, standing up.

26-29 And you shall make bars of acacia wood.…And the middle bar shall pass through in the center of the boards from end to end. And you shall overlay the boards with gold, and make their rings of gold as holders for the bars; and you shall overlay the bars with gold.

Eph. With all lowliness and meekness, with
4:2-3 long-suffering, bearing one another in love, being diligent to keep the oneness of the Spirit in the uniting bond of peace.

_____
Date

Week 9 — Day 3　　Today's verses

John That they all may be one; even as You, Fa-
17:21-23 ther, are in Me and I in You, that they also may be in Us.…That they may be one, even as We are one; I in them, and You in Me, that they may be perfected into one.…

Exo. And you shall make the boards for the
26:15 tabernacle of acacia wood, standing up.

28 And the middle bar shall pass through in the center of the boards from end to end.

Eph. In whom all the building, being fitted
2:21-22 together, is growing into a holy temple in the Lord; in whom you also are being built together into a dwelling place of God in spirit.

_____
Date

Week 10 — Day 4 — Today's verses

1 Cor. 12:12-13   For even as the body is one and has many members, yet all the members of the body, being many, are one body, so also is the Christ. For also in one Spirit we were all baptized into one Body, whether Jews or Greeks, whether slaves or free, and were all given to drink one Spirit.

Eph. 4:12   For the perfecting of the saints unto the work of the ministry, unto the building up of the Body of Christ.

Week 10 — Day 5 — Today's verses

Eph. 4:4   One Body and one Spirit, even as also you were called in one hope of your calling.

1 Cor. 10:16-17   The cup of blessing which we bless, is it not the fellowship of the blood of Christ? The bread which we break, is it not the fellowship of the body of Christ? Seeing that there is one bread, we who are many are one Body; for we all partake of the one bread.

Col. 4:16   And when this letter is read among you, cause that it be read in the church of the Laodiceans also, and that you also read the one from Laodicea.

Week 10 — Day 6 — Today's verses

Rev. 1:11-12   …What you see write in a scroll and send *it* to the seven churches: to Ephesus and to Smyrna….And I turned to see the voice that spoke with me; and when I turned, I saw seven golden lampstands.

21:2   And I saw the holy city, New Jerusalem, coming down out of heaven from God, prepared as a bride adorned for her husband.

Week 10 — Day 1 — Today's verses

Eph. 2:21-22   In whom all the building, being fitted together, is growing into a holy temple in the Lord; in whom you also are being built together into a dwelling place of God in spirit.

1 Cor. 14:12   So also you, since you are zealous of spirits, seek that you may excel for the building up of the church.

Week 10 — Day 2 — Today's verses

Col. 2:19   And not holding the Head, out from whom all the Body…grows with the growth of God.

3:10-11   And have put on the new man, which is being renewed unto full knowledge according to the image of Him who created him, where there cannot be Greek and Jew, circumcision and uncircumcision, barbarian, Scythian, slave, free man, but Christ is all and in all.

Week 10 — Day 3 — Today's verses

Eph. 1:17   That the God of our Lord Jesus Christ, the Father of glory, may give to you a spirit of wisdom and revelation in the full knowledge of Him.

22-23   And He subjected all things under His feet and gave Him *to be* Head over all things to the church, which is His Body, the fullness of the One who fills all in all.

Rom. 12:5   So we who are many are one Body in Christ, and individually members one of another.

Week 11 — Day 4   Today's verses

1 Cor. The work of each will become manifest;
3:13-15 for the day will declare it, because it is revealed by fire, and the fire itself will prove each one's work, of what sort it is. If anyone's work which he has built upon the foundation remains, he will receive a reward; if anyone's work is consumed, he will suffer loss, but he himself will be saved, yet so as through fire.

Matt. And then I will declare to them: I never
7:23 knew you. Depart from Me, you workers of lawlessness.

Date

Week 11 — Day 5   Today's verses

1 Tim. Even as I exhorted you...to remain in
1:3-4 Ephesus in order that you might charge certain ones not to teach different things nor to give heed to myths and unending genealogies, which produce questionings rather than God's economy, which is in faith.

Date

Week 11 — Day 6   Today's verses

Rom. Now I exhort you, brothers, to mark those
16:17 who make divisions and causes of stumbling contrary to the teaching which you have learned, and turn away from them.

Gal. And this, because of the false brothers,
2:4 brought in secretly, who stole in to spy out our freedom which we have in Christ Jesus, that they might bring us into slavery.

Date

Week 11 — Day 1   Today's verses

1 Cor. ...I have laid a foundation, and another
3:10-13 builds upon it. But let each man take heed how he builds upon it. For another foundation no one is able to lay besides that which is laid, which is Jesus Christ. But if anyone builds upon the foundation gold, silver, precious stones, wood, grass, stubble, the work of each will become manifest...of what sort it is.

17 If anyone destroys the temple of God, God will destroy him; for the temple of God is holy, and such are you.

Date

Week 11 — Day 2   Today's verses

1 Cor. For another foundation no one is able to
3:11-12 lay besides that which is laid, which is Jesus Christ. But if anyone builds upon the foundation gold, silver, precious stones, wood, grass, stubble.

Date

Week 11 — Day 3   Today's verses

1 Cor. Do you not know that you are the temple
3:16-17 of God, and that the Spirit of God dwells in you? If anyone destroys the temple of God, God will destroy him; for the temple of God is holy, and such are you.

Date

Week 12 — Day 4   Today's verses

Heb. 1:5   For to which of the angels has He ever said, "You are My Son; this day have I begotten You"?....

John 14:23   ...If anyone loves Me, he will keep My word, and My Father will love him, and We will come to him and make an abode with him.

_____
Date

Week 12 — Day 5   Today's verses

2 Sam. 7:12, 14   ...I will raise up your seed after you....I will be his Father, and he will be My son....

Matt. 22:42-43   Saying, What do you think concerning the Christ? Whose son is He? They said to Him, David's. He said to them, How then does David in spirit call Him Lord...

45   If then David calls Him Lord, how is He his son?

_____
Date

Week 12 — Day 6   Today's verses

Rev. 21:2   And I saw the holy city, New Jerusalem, coming down out of heaven from God, prepared as a bride adorned for her husband.

11   Having the glory of God. Her light was like a most precious stone, like a jasper stone, as clear as crystal.

18-19   ...And the city was pure gold, like clear glass. The foundations of the wall of the city were adorned with every precious stone...

21   And the twelve gates were twelve pearls...

_____
Date

Week 12 — Day 1   Today's verses

2 Sam. 7:12-14   When your days are fulfilled and you sleep with your fathers, I will raise up your seed after you, which will come forth from your body, and I will establish his kingdom. It is he who will build a house for My name, and I will establish the throne of his kingdom forever. I will be his Father, and he will be My son....

Eph. 3:17   That Christ may make His home in your hearts through faith...

_____
Date

Week 12 — Day 2   Today's verses

1 Cor. 3:12   But if anyone builds upon the foundation gold, silver, precious stones, wood, grass, stubble.

Eph. 4:12   For the perfecting of the saints unto the work of the ministry, unto the building up of the Body of Christ.

16   ...All the Body...causes the growth of the Body unto the building up of itself in love.

Matt. 16:18   ...I will build My church...

_____
Date

Week 12 — Day 3   Today's verses

2 Sam. 7:12-14   When your days are fulfilled and you sleep with your fathers, I will raise up your seed after you, which will come forth from your body, and I will establish his kingdom. It is he who will build a house for My name, and I will establish the throne of his kingdom forever. I will be his Father, and he will be My son....

Rom. 1:3-4   Concerning His Son, who came out of the seed of David according to the flesh, who was designated the Son of God in power according to the Spirit of holiness out of the resurrection of the dead, Jesus Christ our Lord.

_____
Date